Early Praise for *Core Data in Swift*

Marcus's books have long been my go-to recommendation for people who want to learn about Core Data. With new information for beginners and experts alike, they are a great insight into how you should be using Core Data and the features that it offers.

➤ **Daniel Tomlinson**
  Senior software engineer, Rocket Apps Ltd.

Marcus has a profound understanding of Core Data, and this book describes not only the basics of working with Core Data, but also how to do so in a performant manner, with explanations and examples. This is an indispensable reference, alongside Apple's documentation, and one that will quickly make Core Data your go-to persistence mechanism. You'll be able to deal with anything that comes up with confidence.

➤ **Abizer Nasir**
  Lead developer, Jungle Candy Software Ltd.

A compelling book, packed with useful information.

➤ **Steven Oxley**
  Senior engineer, Social Native

Core Data in Swift

Data Storage and Management for iOS and OS X

Marcus S. Zarra

The Pragmatic Bookshelf

Raleigh, North Carolina

Many of the designations used by manufacturers and sellers to distinguish their products are claimed as trademarks. Where those designations appear in this book, and The Pragmatic Programmers, LLC was aware of a trademark claim, the designations have been printed in initial capital letters or in all capitals. The Pragmatic Starter Kit, The Pragmatic Programmer, Pragmatic Programming, Pragmatic Bookshelf, PragProg and the linking *g* device are trademarks of The Pragmatic Programmers, LLC.

Every precaution was taken in the preparation of this book. However, the publisher assumes no responsibility for errors or omissions, or for damages that may result from the use of information (including program listings) contained herein.

Our Pragmatic books, screencasts, and audio books can help you and your team create better software and have more fun. Visit us at *https://pragprog.com*.

The team that produced this book includes:

Jacquelyn Carter (editor)
Potomac Indexing, LLC (index)
Liz Welch (copyedit)
Gilson Graphics (layout)
Janet Furlow (producer)

For sales, volume licensing, and support, please contact *support@pragprog.com*.

For international rights, please contact *rights@pragprog.com*.

Printed in the United States of America.
ISBN-13: 978-1-68050-170-4
Printed on acid-free paper.
Book version: P1.0—June 2016

Contents

Introduction

It's amazing to realize that as of the writing of this book, Core Data is over 12 years old. That's an incredible number when you consider that it's more powerful and more popular today than it has ever been. For a framework, that's pretty spectacular.

In this book we discuss Core Data and work with the framework from the perspective of Swift. Swift is a young language and has a lot of growing yet to do, but its popularity can't be denied.

It's clear that Swift is important to Apple and therefore should be equally important to developers who work on Apple's platforms.

Is This Book for You?

If you plan on writing an application that saves data to disk, then you should take a very long look at Core Data. Whether you're focusing on the desktop or the iPhone, Core Data is the most efficient solution to data persistence.

A good way to confirm that you know enough Cocoa to benefit from this book is to take a look at Chapter 1, *Before We Begin*, on page 1. You should find it dense, but every step should be familiar to you.

What Is Core Data?

In the simplest terms, Core Data is an object graph that can be persisted to disk. But just like describing a man as a "bag of mostly water," that description hardly does Core Data justice. If you have worked with Interface Builder (specifically on OS X), you know that it effectively removes a third of the coding from the Model-View-Controller (MVC) design pattern. With Interface Builder, developers don't need to spend countless hours writing and rewriting their user interface to make sure that it's pixel perfect. Instead, they simply drag and drop the elements in the IDE, bind them together, and call it done.

Of course, the problem with Interface Builder is that we still need to code the other two parts! Both the controller and the model need to be developed in code and made to work with the interface we just designed. That's where Core Data comes in. In a nutshell, Core Data deals with a third of that MVC design: Core Data is the model.

It is a common misconception that Core Data is a database API for Cocoa that allows a Cocoa application to store its data in a database. Although that description is factually accurate, Core Data does a lot more. It serves as the entire model layer. It's not just the persistence on disk; it's also all the objects in memory that we normally consider to be data objects. If you have experience working with Java, C#, or some other object-oriented language, the data objects take a lot of time to write, and they're generally very repetitive in nature. Core Data eliminates most, if not all, of that boilerplate code for us and lets us focus on the business logic, or the controller layer, of our application. It does this with an interface that's as easy to use as Interface Builder.

In addition to ease of use, Core Data is highly flexible. If we need to step in and change the functionality of some portion of the data model, we can. From how a value is handled when it's being accessed to how data is migrated from one persistent store to another, we can choose how little or how much we want to code ourselves and how much we want Core Data to do for us.

When you start to learn Core Data, it's best to think in terms of objects. Core Data is a framework designed to manage your data and data object graph. As a secondary function, it will persist that data to disk. However, its primary function is to manage the objects.

Online Resources

The app and examples shown in this book can be found at the Pragmatic Programmers website for this book.[1] You'll also find the community forum and the errata-submission form, where you can report problems with the text or make suggestions for future versions.

---

1. http://pragprog.com/book/mzswift/core-data-in-swift

CHAPTER 1

Before We Begin

This is a book with two beginnings and one ending. The ending should be obvious: to increase your knowledge and understanding of Core Data.

Of the two beginnings, you get to choose. If you're relatively new to either iOS development or Swift, then please read this chapter; it was written for you.

If, on the other hand, you're intimately familiar with iOS—perhaps you even prefer to build your test cases in your own way—then I suggest you jump to Chapter 2, *Under the Hood*, on page 13. The chapter you're currently reading focuses on building a test application.

Test Application

When you're learning how to write software using Swift or when you're first learning how to develop an iOS application, the book that's helping you generally starts at zero, often referred to as the "Hello World" application.

This is not that kind of book. For us to explore Core Data a certain level of knowledge is necessary—a foundation of knowledge that we can build upon.

This book expects that you understand the fundamentals of Swift. It's written in a such a way that you don't need to be a master of Swift. We aren't going to be doing any complex coding using the unusual bits of Swift. We're intentionally avoiding those.

The focus of this book is to increase your knowledge of Core Data while working in the Swift environment. Therefore, the code is as straightforward as I can make it.

On our journey to learn about Core Data, we're going to use an original iPhone recipe application. While the application itself is fairly complex and contains a large number of views, the concepts behind these views are standard and will be familiar to anyone who has done work in Cocoa. If you haven't yet mastered Swift and Cocoa, then I highly suggest you review Chris Adamson and Janie Clayton's *iOS 9 SDK Development*, published by the Pragmatic Bookshelf.

Our goal in this chapter is to establish a baseline application from which to work. Core Data is a supporting framework, and we need something for it to support in order to explore and demonstrate its features and characteristics. This recipe application is the foundation used in the book. You can use this chapter as a reference of the overall picture of the application as we're exploring the inner workings of Core Data in the rest of the chapters.

If you're already comfortable with storyboards and the creation of iOS applications, feel free to skim the provided code sample and jump to Chapter 2, *Under the Hood*, on page 13, in which we'll begin to dive into the substance of Core Data.

The Transmission of a Car

When I describe Core Data to nonprogrammers, I tend to use a car analogy.

If you were a car mechanic and wanted to learn how to work on transmissions, you'd buy a book that was specific to transmissions. However, that book wouldn't teach you how to build a car; it'd dive right into the workings and theories of a transmission.

The differences between car mechanics and programming show up right away. The author of the book can be reasonably certain that the reader will have access to a car and that it is already going to have a transmission built in that the reader can use to apply the knowledge from the book. This isn't necessarily true in programming.

Since I can't be certain that you have an application in your possession that contains Core Data already, I'm including one with this book. This chapter gives you a car to tinker with while we explore the transmission.

The Storyboard

To keep the structure of our application as simple as possible, we'll use a *storyboard* to design the entire UI of our iPhone application. As you'll recall from your reading or experience, a storyboard allows us to view the entire application interaction in one place. We can also control a greater portion of the UI within the storyboard and thus allow for even less code to be introduced to our project. You can see a zoomed-out version of our storyboard in the following screenshot on page 3.

What Is a Storyboard?

When non-Apple developers think of storyboards, they think of playing with application flow and designs—probably on a napkin or a whiteboard. However, with Apple's development tools, the word "storyboard" has a different meaning.

Within Xcode is a visual design tool called Interface Builder. Interface Builder can produce a file referred to as a "storyboard." These storyboards can be all or part of an application's user interface. It's possible for every visual element within an application to be stored inside a single storyboard file.

These storyboard files get compiled into the application and are used when the application is run to display the user interface. They're the latest iteration of Apple's user interface tool that previously produced "nib" and "xib" files.

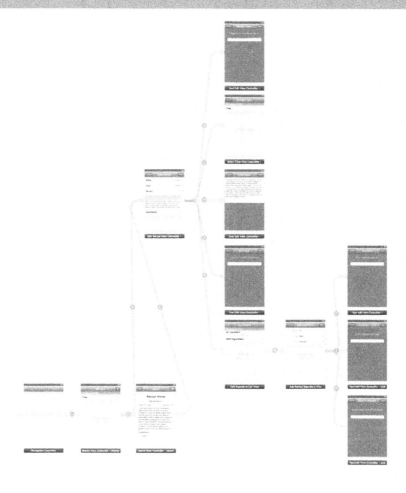

This storyboard seems complex—and it is. However, most of the code needed to support these views is minimal, and there's a fair amount of view controller reuse that will make the application easier to develop and maintain.

There are three primary elements to this application: a list of recipes, a detailed view of a single recipe, and the ability to add/edit recipes. The add/edit feature is the most complex, so we'll save it for last.

> ## The Source Code
>
> To avoid making you copy the code and designs out of this book, all of the source code is available for download at www.pragprog.com.

The Recipe List

When users launch our application, they're immediately presented with a list of recipes. The list is represented in the storyboard as a UITableView with a prototype cell. We're using a basic cell in the prototype, as shown here.

Associated with this UI element in the storyboard, we also have a UIViewController named PPRMasterViewController. The data for this UITableViewController is driven by an NSFetchedResultsController (which we explore in detail in Chapter 3, *iOS: NSFetchedResultsController*, on page 33). Right now we're concerned with the segues of this UIViewController. The segues describe the transition that our application uses when going from one view controller to another. A segue can happen when we select a row in a table, a button in the navigation bar, a button on the tab bar, or virtually anything that causes the UI to move to another view controller.

PPRecipes/PPRecipes/PPRMasterViewController.swift

```swift
override func prepareForSegue(segue: UIStoryboardSegue, sender: AnyObject?) {
  guard let identifier = segue.identifier else {
    fatalError("Unidentified segue")
  }

  switch identifier {
  case "showRecipe":
    prepareForDetailSegue(segue)
  case "addRecipe":
    prepareForAddRecipeSegue(segue)
  default:
    fatalError("Unexpected segue: \(identifier)")
  }
}
```

When a segue is activated, the current UIViewController receives a call to prepare-
ForSegue(: sender:). That's our opportunity to prepare the next UIViewController for
display. It's a good idea to use this method as a branching point for each
potential segue. Taking this step aids with code clarity and maintenance.
With one or two segues, this method is fairly easy to maintain. However, when
we have many possible segues, the code quickly becomes unwieldy. Instead
of waiting for the code to become unwieldy and refactoring it, we start off by
using this method as a branching point.

PPRecipes/PPRecipes/PPRMasterViewController.swift

```swift
func prepareForDetailSegue(segue: UIStoryboardSegue) {
  let control = segue.destinationViewController as! PPRDetailViewController
  let path = tableView.indexPathForSelectedRow!
  let recipe = fResultsController!.objectAtIndexPath(path) as! PPRRecipeMO
  control.recipeMO = recipe
}
```

The first segue brings in the PPRDetailViewController and displays a single recipe
in detail. The method prepareForDetailSegue(:) demonstrates the *dependency
injection pattern*. We obtain a reference to the about-to-be exposed UIViewController, and we *inject* the information that it needs. We'll use this pattern
extensively throughout the book.

PPRecipes/PPRecipes/PPRMasterViewController.swift

```swift
func prepareForAddRecipeSegue(segue: UIStoryboardSegue) {
  let tempController = segue.destinationViewController
  let controller = tempController as! PPREditRecipeViewController
  let moc = managedObjectContext!
  let recipe = NSEntityDescription.insertNewObjectForEntityForName("Recipe",
    inManagedObjectContext: moc) as! PPRRecipeMO
  controller.recipeMO = recipe
}
```

The second segue branches us into the editing capabilities of our application. This is our first bit of code reuse.

Instead of having an "add" logic path and an "edit" logic path, the paths are combined. In fact, their functionality is 99 percent identical. The 1 percent difference between them concerns whether an object is being created or an existing object is being edited. By again using dependency injection, we pull that 1 percent difference out of the logic path and let the parent UIViewController make the decision. As far as the rest of our editing workflow is concerned, there's no difference. It's being handed a data object, and it doesn't matter whether the object has been created anew or whether it previously existed.

The Recipe Detail

When users select a recipe in our application, we want to display everything about the recipe in one screen so they can easily absorb the information and prepare the recipe. We'll need one fairly complex UIViewController in order to give them that one-screen access. Take a look at the following screenshot for a sample of the view.

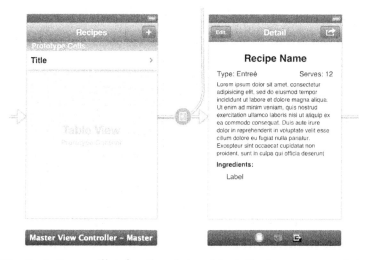

In our UIViewController, we'll take the data object that was passed to us and display it in one (potentially) lengthy UIScrollView.

The edit button in the UINavigationBar is the interesting part of this view controller. When the edit button is tapped, we enter the edit workflow (we'll discuss this further in the next section). This process is identical to the add workflow we discussed in *The Recipe List*, on page 4. With this code reuse, we can now enter the same workflow from the view controller that allows us to view a recipe as we did from the list recipes view controller. Both of these produce the same effect: we can edit a recipe, and it doesn't matter if that recipe is new or existing.

PPRecipes/PPRecipes/PPRDetailViewController.swift

```
override func prepareForSegue(segue: UIStoryboardSegue, sender: AnyObject?) {
  guard let identifier = segue.identifier else {
    fatalError("Unidentified segue")
  }
  assert(identifier == "editRecipe", "Unexpected identifier: \(identifier)")

  let controller = segue.destinationViewController
    as! PPREditRecipeViewController

  controller.recipeMO = recipeMO
}
```

Note the subtle difference in this reuse. In the previous version of the edit workflow, we created a new data object. In this version, we take our existing reference to the data object and hand it off to the edit workflow.

The Edit Workflow

The complexity of our application really lives in the edit workflow shown here. It is in this workflow that we edit, delete, and change data objects.

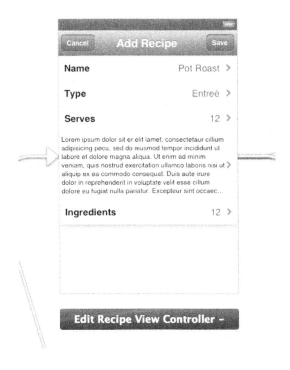

The bulk of the complexity of the edit workflow is in the very first UIViewController. To begin with, this UITable ViewController uses static cells, as opposed to prototype cells. In this design, we have a known quantity of cells, and each cell displays a different piece of information.

By utilizing static cells, we do a significant portion of the work of the edit workflow directly in the storyboard. We avoid handling a large amount of complexity in our application when a user selects a cell. In other words, instead of having to figure out which cell was selected, determine the view controller to build, populate that view controller, present it, and so on, we can have the storyboard do the bulk of that work for us. Each cell in this UITableViewController has a segue to another UIViewController. Each of those segues is named, and we can therefore do away with a large portion of code. Our UITableViewController subclass needs to look only at the identifier of the segue and inject the right dependencies.

PPRecipes/PPRecipes/PPREditRecipeViewController.swift

```swift
override func prepareForSegue(segue: UIStoryboardSegue, sender: AnyObject?) {
  guard let identifier = segue.identifier else {
    fatalError("Unidentified segue")
  }

  switch identifier {
  case "editRecipeName":
    prepareForEditRecipeNameSegue(segue.destinationViewController)
  case "selectRecipeType":
    prepareForSelectTypeSegue(segue.destinationViewController)
  case "selectNumberOfServings":
    prepareForSetServingsSegue(segue.destinationViewController)
  case "selectLastUsed":
    prepareForSetDateSegue(segue.destinationViewController)
  case "selectAuthor":
    prepareForSelectAuthorSegue(segue.destinationViewController)
  case "selectIngredients":
    prepareForSelectIngredientSegue(segue.destinationViewController)
  case "editDescription":
    prepareForDirectionsSegue(segue.destinationViewController)
  default:
    fatalError("Unrecognized segue: \(identifier)")
  }
}
```

Here we see the value of using the -prepareForSegue: sender: method only for branching. Had we put all of the flow logic into this one method, it would easily be 100 lines of code or more and be a mess to maintain.

All of the UIViewController instances that are accessed from the edit UITableViewController fall into one of two categories: edit something or select something. Let's look at an example of both kinds of instance. See the following screenshot.

Text Edit View Controller

The PPRTextEditViewController is easily the most reused UIViewController. The bulk of a recipe is text, and the text is probably going to need to be edited. As a result, the process of editing in our application must be highly reusable. This is also a great opportunity to use a block callback to assist in the reusability of the PPRTextEditViewController.

PPRecipes/PPRecipes/PPREditRecipeViewController.swift

```swift
func prepareForEditRecipeNameSegue(ac: UIViewController) {
  guard let controller = ac as? PPRTextEditViewController else {
    fatalError("Unexpected controller type")
  }
  controller.text = recipeMO?.valueForKey("name") as? String

  controller.textChangedClosure = { (text: String) in
    self.recipeMO?.setValue(text, forKey: "name")
    let path = NSIndexPath(forRow: 0, inSection: 0)
    let cell = self.tableView.cellForRowAtIndexPath(path)
    cell?.detailTextLabel?.text = text
  }
}
```

The most interesting part of this segue preparation is the callback. The PPR-TextEditViewController is actually quite dumb. Its entire job is to consume the text entered into a text field and listen for either the Done button to be clicked or the Return key to be tapped. When either of those happen, it takes the text from the UITextField (or the UITextView) and passes it to the callback block.

Note that the block accepts a string and expects the closure to throw an error if it's appropriate. The parent, which defines the block, then validates the text and throws the error if there's a problem. The PPRTextEditViewController receives a pass/fail from the block. In the event of a failure, it displays the error. If the block returns a pass, the text view controller pops back to its parent.

With this design, we can use the PPRTextEditViewController to edit any piece of text we choose, and it doesn't need any custom or special handling code. The only thing we need to do for each instance is set up its view in the storyboard and pass in the text that it needs to start with. By customizing the view, we also gain access to which keyboard is appropriate for each text edit, thereby making it easy to reuse this UIViewController for numeric text, email addresses, or virtually any data we can think of.

The second function of the callback block is to update the data object and the edit view. Since we're using static cells, we must grab a reference to the existing cell and refresh it based on the text being passed into the block.

List Ingredients View Controller

While there are a couple of "select something" items in the PPREditRecipeViewController, the ingredients selection is by far the most interesting. First, we want to display all of the existing ingredients. To do this, we need a selection view controller. Next, we want to add ingredients, which means we have to add an Add Ingredient row when the user taps the Edit button. When users select the Add Ingredient row, we put them into another view controller that allows them to edit the individual components of an ingredient. In the Add Ingredient view, we allow users to set the quantity, type of ingredient, and unit of measure. The end result can be seen in the following screenshot on page 11.

Later, as we update and enhance our application, this workflow becomes even longer and more complicated. Fortunately, the code stays quite sane with the reuse of view controllers and the use of the storyboard.

Unfortunately, we need to build two specific view controllers for this workflow: one to handle listing the ingredients (including adding and deleting) and one for adding an ingredient. Luckily, we can get a lot of reuse from our text edit view controller in this part of the application.

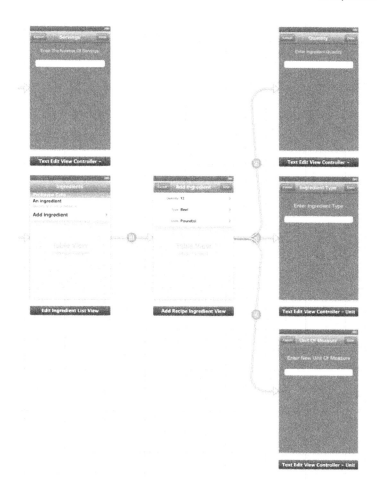

Ready for Core Data

The story now merges from the two beginnings. In the next chapter we'll dive into the structural components of Core Data, walk through each of the pieces, and see how they fit into the puzzle.

At the end of that chapter, you'll have a firm understanding of the Core Data stack and how to access it. From there we'll begin to utilize some of the more advanced concepts behind Core Data to improve on our application.

You can download the source code for this application (and the future changes we're going to introduce) at PragProg.com.[1]

---

1. http://www.pragprog.com

CHAPTER 2

Under the Hood

In the previous chapter you may have read about the application we'll be using as our structure for most of the rest of the book. If you're the type who prefers to build your own test cases and/or have extensive experience building iOS applications, then you've most likely skipped ahead to this chapter. Even so, the first chapter is a good reference to see how the baseline application used throughout this book was developed.

Part of the barrier to entering the world of Core Data is that it's perceived as having a steep learning curve. Looking at the code samples that Apple provides for developers, you might at first glance agree with that evaluation. That perception was born from the first few iterations of the framework. When Core Data was first introduced, there was a large amount of confusion over what needs to be done, what doesn't need to be done, and what we're allowed to do with the framework. A lot has changed since those early days. As you'll see in the next couple of chapters, Core Data is very easy to use, and when you need the complexity to handle an edge case, the options are available.

In my experience of working with and writing persistence layers for various languages, I'm constantly amazed at how simple and elegant the Core Data API is. There's very little overlap in functionality between the individual pieces of Core Data—no wasted space or unnecessary redundancy. Because Core Data is built on the infrastructure of Objective-C (Core Data hasn't been rewritten into Swift yet) and Core Foundation, it doesn't seek to duplicate functionality that already exists in other parts of the overall API but instead uses that functionality to its fullest extent.

In this chapter, we go through the key pieces of Core Data and remove some of the mysticism that surrounds them. By the end of this chapter, you'll have a much higher comfort level and will be able to understand what all of that sample code does. We'll also be discussing the terminology of Core Data so that you can better understand what the individual components are and how they work together.

At its most basic level, Core Data is an object graph designed to manage data objects. It's common when you're first approaching Core Data to think of it as an object-relational mapping framework—and in truth, it can be used as such. However, that isn't the best approach. My elevator pitch for Core Data goes like this: "Core Data is an object graph that *can* persist to a database." The primary function of Core Data is to *manage* the object graph. Persisting the data to disk is a secondary, although vital, function.

The Core Data API, or *stack* as it's commonly called, consists of three primary pieces: the NSManagedObjectModel, the NSPersistentStoreCoordinator, and the NSManagedObjectContext, as shown here.

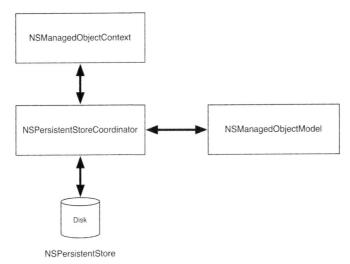

All of these pieces work together to allow a program to retrieve and store NSManagedObject instances. In most situations, the program will access the NSManagedObjectContext only once the stack has been created. It's possible to access the other components of the stack, but it's rarely necessary. Each of the three pieces of the Core Data stack work together. As we'll review in detail, the NSManagedObjectModel feeds structure to the NSPersistentStoreCoordinator and the NSPersistentStoreCoordinator feeds data and structure to the NSManagedObjectContext. The NSManagedObjectContext in turn handles requests from the rest of the application to create, update, delete, and insert NSManagedObject instances.

Throughout this chapter, and most of the rest of the book, we'll be referencing the application that we built in Chapter 1, *Before We Begin*, on page 1. We'll start that reference by exploring the creation of the Core Data stack.

Introducing the NSManagedObjectModel

The first part of our exploration of the components of Core Data is the portion of the framework that's the least accessed: the NSManagedObjectModel. An object model is a way to describe the data in terms of objects. The NSManagedObjectModel is a compiled, binary version of the data model that we create graphically in Xcode. When we say that we're manipulating the object model, we mean we're editing the source file in Xcode that will get compiled and used by the NSManagedObjectModel. From a database perspective, this file represents the schema of the database. In Xcode, this file is shown in two different styles; the easiest to recognize is shown here.

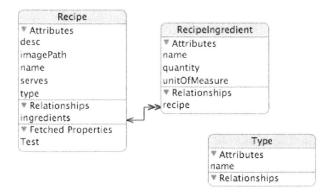

While this view is great for conceptualizing the data and the objects, it's not great for editing. Therefore, the style can be changed using a control in the lower-right corner called Editor Style. The second style is shown here.

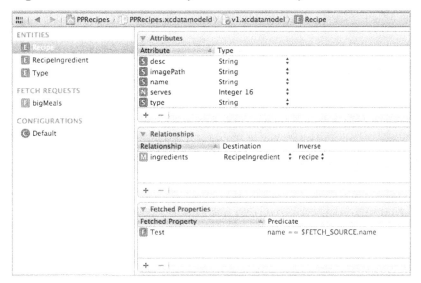

The NSManagedObjectModel—and, by extension, the associated source file in the object model—is what we think of when we need to change the object model. The source file is saved as an xcdatamodel file. That file is stored within a Cocoa style bundle that starts out with the same filename. If you were to look at the file structure directly you would see a folder with the xcdatamodeld extension and then you'd find the actual data model file inside. The reason for this structure is explained in Chapter 4, *Versioning and Migration*, on page 47.

Xcode understands how to compile these files in this bundle. When Xcode encounters these files during the compile process of a project, it compiles them into a binary form ending with the extension mom inside of a bundle with the momd extension. We can also build these files from the command line using the momc tool.

Editing the Data Model

In Chapter 1, *Before We Begin*, on page 1, the sample project started with the data model already created. Let's look at how that that data model was created. To begin with, we told Xcode to create a new file (File > New > File...), and we selected Data Model from the template, as shown here.

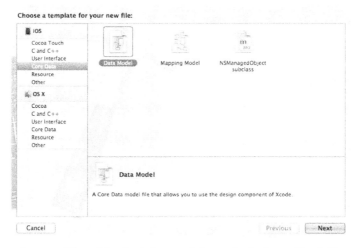

This presents us with a blank data model ready to be edited. From here, in grid view, we added the three entities being used in the project: Recipe, RecipeIngredient, and Type. We then added the attributes and relationships for each of those entities. For a discussion of entities, attributes, and relationships, take a look at *Working with NSManagedObject Instances*, on page 21.

Loading the Data Model

Once we've created the source file for the data model, we need to instantiate it within our application. In the Xcode sample projects, this is generally done in its own method in the application's AppDelegate. However, this process is unnecessary and tends to add to code bloat in the AppDelegate. My preference is to treat Core Data, really the entire persistence layer, as a first-class citizen in the application. What this means is that we can create a new controller that's a subclass of NSObject and place all of the Core Data–related code into that controller. From there we can instantiate that controller within the Application Delegate.

Further, I like to construct the entire Core Data stack in a single method. There's rarely a situation where you wish to build only part of the stack. With that structure, you can kick off the initialization of the Core Data stack as soon as the application launches so that it's available, in some form, immediately. Therefore, in our sample application, we have a method named -initializeCoreDataStack that starts off with constructing the data model.

PPRecipes/PPRecipes/PPRDataController.swift

```
func initializeCoreDataStack() {
  guard let modelURL = NSBundle.mainBundle().URLForResource("PPRecipes",
    withExtension: "momd") else {
    fatalError("Failed to locate DataModel.momd in app bundle")
  }
  guard let mom = NSManagedObjectModel(contentsOfURL: modelURL) else {
    fatalError("Failed to initialize MOM")
  }
```

To initialize the NSManagedObjectModel, we first need to locate it within the application bundle. We call on the NSBundle and retrieve the -mainBundle, which represents the application bundle. From there, we call -URLForResource: withExtension: using the name of our data model—in this case PPRecipes—and the extension momd. We use a guard to verify that we did receive an NSURL. We then initialize the NSManagedObjectModel with that NSURL. We again verify that everything worked correctly by using a guard against the initialization.

And that's everything involved in constructing the NSManagedObjectModel. Our next step is to construct the NSPersistentStoreCoordinator, which uses the NSManagedObjectModel we just initialized.

Integrating with the NSPersistentStoreCoordinator

The NSPersistentStoreCoordinator is the true maestro of Core Data. The NSPersistentStoreCoordinator is responsible for persisting, loading, and caching data. Think of the NSPersistentStoreCoordinator as the heart of Core Data. Having said this, we do very little work with the NSPersistentStoreCoordinator directly. We work with it upon initialization, but we almost never touch it again over the life of the application.

As part of our initialization, we perform two steps with the NSPersistentStoreCoordinator. First, we initialize it, which requires a valid NSManagedObjectModel. Once it's initialized, we add one or more NSPersistentStore instances. An NSPersistentStore is a representation of a location in which the data is saved/persisted. Typically, this persistence is done to disk. However, that step isn't required; it could be in memory or even over the network. For now, let's focus on disk persistence. The NSPersistentStore is responsible for describing the file format used. This file format can be one of several: SQLite, binary, or atomic. (There's also an XML store for OS X, but I don't recommend using it because it isn't available on iOS, nor does it perform very well.) To keep our focus, we'll use the SQLite format in this first iteration of our application and explore the other formats later in the book.

In previous versions of Core Data and the sample projects, the initialization of the NSPersistentStoreCoordinator and the addition of the NSPersistentStore were done in a single method. This example tended to lead to a number of issues for developers because they didn't fully understand the impact of the example. Therefore, we're going to do this initialization in a more complex way, but it will be a way that won't paint us into a corner.

PPRecipes/PPRecipes/PPRDataController.swift

```
let psc = NSPersistentStoreCoordinator(managedObjectModel: mom)
```

In this first bit of code, we initialize the NSPersistentStoreCoordinator and pass it the NSManagedObjectModel that we previously initialized. This call returns immediately, therefore we can do it in line as part of the startup of the application.

Adding one or more NSPersistentStore instances to the NSPersistentStoreCoordinator, however, can take an unknown amount of time. The reason for the unpredictability is that we could also be performing a migration during the call (as discussed in Chapter 4, *Versioning and Migration*, on page 47), or we could be linking and updating with iCloud (as discussed in Chapter 9, *Using Core Data with iCloud*, on page 123). If either of those situations occurs, the addition of the NSPersistentStore can delay the launch of the application to the point of providing a poor user experience or, worse, being terminated by the operating system. To avoid either of these situations, we want to add the NSPersistentStore on a background queue so that the application can finish launching while we perform our startup.

```
let queue = dispatch_get_global_queue(DISPATCH_QUEUE_PRIORITY_DEFAULT, 0)
dispatch_async(queue) {
  let fileManager = NSFileManager.defaultManager()
  guard let documentsURL = fileManager.URLsForDirectory(.DocumentDirectory,
    inDomains: .UserDomainMask).first else {
    fatalError("Failed to resolve documents directory")
  }
  let storeURL = documentsURL.URLByAppendingPathComponent("PPRecipes.sqlite")

  do {
    try psc.addPersistentStoreWithType(NSSQLiteStoreType,
      configuration: nil, URL: storeURL, options: nil)
  } catch {
    fatalError("Failed to initialize PSC: \(error)")
  }
```

In this portion of the code, we grab a reference to a global queue with a default priority. Then we add a block to be executed on that queue that will handle the addition of the NSPersistentStore to the NSPersistentStoreCoordinator.

Inside that block, we first determine where we want to store the file associated with our NSPersistentStore. In this example, we're going to put it into the Documents directory that's part of the application sandbox. If we were working on OS X, we could put it in the Application Support folder or anywhere else that was appropriate. We resolve this path using the NSFileManager and call its URLsForDirectory(: inDomains:) method, which will return an array of NSURL instances. We call last on that array to retrieve the last NSURL. We then append the filename for our NSPersistentStore to the end of that NSURL.

With the location of the store now resolved, we can add the NSPersistentStore to the NSPersistentStoreCoordinator. We do this with a call to addPersistentStoreWithType(: configuration: URL: options:). This is a complex method call, so let's break it down by parameter. There are four in all.

- The first parameter is Type. This tells the NSPersistentStoreCoordinator what type of store we want initialized. In this case, we're passing NSSQLiteStoreType to indicate we want a SQLite store. This is the parameter to change if we want to use another store type.

- The second parameter is configuration. This is an advanced setting that allows us to partition our data model into different configurations for different uses. Since we aren't partitioning our data model at this time, we'll pass nil, which tells the NSPersistentStoreCoordinator that we want to use the default configuration.

- The third parameter, URL, accepts the NSURL for the store. We pass in the NSURL that we resolved earlier.

- The fourth parameter, options, allows us to change the behavior of the NSPersistentStore. This parameter is used during versioning, during iCloud configuration, and for on-disk encryption. We aren't using any of these features at this time, so we pass nil here as well.

This call will either return an NSPersistentStore or throw an error. If it throws an error, that means something failed, and we need to interrogate the error.

Once this call is completed, our NSPersistentStoreCoordinator is fully initialized and ready to be used. Since we've completed this step on a background queue, it's helpful to notify the UI that it's ready to be used. Therefore, we end the block with a call back onto the main queue and allow the UI to complete its initialization. This completion could include removing a modal dialog or even just telling the view controllers to reload themselves. The exact experience is left up to the developer.

PPRecipes/PPRecipes/PPRDataController.swift

```
dispatch_sync(dispatch_get_main_queue()) {
  self.initializationComplete?()
}
```

Once we initialize the NSPersistentStoreCoordinator, we rarely, if ever, access it directly again. It silently works in the background, persisting the data. Because of this, we don't need to keep a reference to it directly; instead, we can rely on the NSManagedObjectContext to do that for us.

Adding the NSManagedObjectContext

Next to NSManagedObject, NSManagedObjectContext is the object in the Core Data stack that we'll most often access. The NSManagedObjectContext is the object we access when we want to save to disk, when we want to read data into memory, and when we want to create new objects. The NSManagedObjectContext is at the top of the Core Data stack in that it's accessed directly by our code frequently. It's much less common for us to need to go deeper into the stack.

NSManagedObjectContext can't be accessed from multiple threads. Each thread that needs access to data should have its own NSManagedObjectContext. This is generally not an issue, since it's very easy to create multiple contexts as needed for data that has to be addressed in the background. Using Core Data in a multithreaded environment is discussed in detail in Chapter 6, *Threading*, on page 79.

PPRecipes/PPRecipes/PPRDataController.swift

```
let type = NSManagedObjectContextConcurrencyType.MainQueueConcurrencyType
mainContext = NSManagedObjectContext(concurrencyType: type)
mainContext?.persistentStoreCoordinator = psc
```

The NSManagedObjectContext itself is fairly straightforward to initialize. The initialization of the NSManagedObjectContext requires a parameter to specify whether it will be used by the user interface. In our first iteration of the Core Data stack, we're creating a single NSManagedObjectContext that will be used by the user interface. Therefore, we pass the parameter NSMainQueueConcurrencyType as part of the initialization of the context so that it will be configured to be used on the main queue. The different types of contexts are discussed in detail in Chapter 6, *Threading*, on page 79.

Once the NSManagedObjectContext has been initialized, we only need to set the NSPersistentStoreCoordinator that it's going to access. From there, it's ready to be used. If you look at our sample application, you'll notice that the order in which these events were described is different from the order they appear in the code. In the code, the NSManagedObjectContext is actually initialized prior to kicking off the block to add the NSPersistentStore to the NSPersistentStoreCoordinator. The reason for this is one of potential order. We want to guarantee that the @property for the NSManagedObjectContext is set before the NSPersistentStore is added and before the -contextInitialized method is called. Although it's highly unlikely that the block on the queue would complete before the method we're in, there's no reason to risk it.

Working with NSManagedObject Instances

The NSManagedObject is the object we work with the most in a Core Data application. Each instance of the NSManagedObject represents one entity in our Core Data repository. By combining Core Data with KVO (Key Value Observing) and KVC (Key Value Coding), this one object can dynamically represent any object that we need and that can be defined in our data model. KVO and KVC are discussed in detail in Chapter 11, *Bindings, KVC, and KVO*, on page 157. To learn more about them, I highly recommend you read Apple's excellent documentation on the subjects.[1]

The properties and relationships defined in our data model are available and are easy to access directly from the NSManagedObject. Without subclassing it, we can access values associated with an NSManagedObject in the following ways.

---

1. https://developer.apple.com/library/ios/documentation/General/Conceptual/DevPedia-CocoaCore/KeyValueCoding.html

Accessing Attributes

Attributes are the easiest to access. By utilizing KVC, we can get or set any attribute on the NSManagedObject directly. If you've reviewed our sample app in Chapter 1, *Before We Begin*, on page 1, you may have noticed that we didn't write a Recipe class. At this point, the NSManagedObject provides all the functionality that we require. For example, we could get the name as follows:

```
let recipe = ...
let name = recipe.valueForKey("name")
```

Likewise, we can set the name in a similar fashion, as follows:

```
let recipe = ...
recipe.setValue("New Name", forKey:"name")
```

When we want to subclass NSManagedObject, we can also define properties for the attributes (and relationships discussed in a moment) so that we can access them directly.

```
@NSManaged var desc: String?
@NSManaged var imagePath: String?
@NSManaged var lastUsed: NSDate?
@NSManaged var name: String?
@NSManaged var serves: Int?
@NSManaged var type: String?
```

As you can see, we're defining the property *almost* like normal, but we're adding a special keyword before each: @NSManaged. Since these properties are created dynamically at runtime, we need to inform the compiler so that it will treat them correctly.

By declaring them with @NSManaged, we're telling the compiler to ignore any warnings associated with these properties because we *promise* to generate them at runtime. Naturally, if they turn up missing at runtime, our application is going to crash. However, when we're working with NSManagedObject objects, the attributes will be looked up for us, therefore we don't need to implement anything. By adding that code, we can access the attribute directly, as shown in the following example:

```
let myRecipe = ...
let recipeName = myRecipe.name
//Do something with the name
myRecipe.name = recipeName
```

No warnings or errors will be generated with this code, and when our application runs we'll be able to access the properties just like any "normal" subclass of NSObject.

Understanding Primitive Access

It should be noted that accessing the attribute via KVC or properties will trigger KVO notifications that the attribute has changed. There are situations where we don't want this to occur or where we prefer it to occur later. In those cases, we can access the attribute using the -primitiveValueForKey: and -setPrimitiveValue:forKey: methods. Both of these methods work the same as the -valueForKey: and -setValue:forKey methods that we're used to working with, but they don't cause KVO notifications to fire. This means the rest of our application will be unaware of any changes we make until and unless we notify it. This is quite useful when you're loading in data from an external source and the data is going to impact several attributes at once. Imagine we wrote a recipe importer that accepted a comma-separated value (CSV) file from another recipe application. In that situation, we might not want the UI or other parts of our application making decisions based on the data in the middle of the import. Therefore, we'd want to update the values without notifications, and once all of them are done, we let the notifications go out. The code to handle this situation would look like this:

```
func importData(values: [String:AnyObject]) {
    willChangeValueForKey("name")
    willChangeValueForKey("desc")
    willChangeValueForKey("serves")
    willChangeValueForKey("type")
    setPrimitiveValue(values["name"], forKey:"name")
    setPrimitiveValue(values["desc"], forKey:"desc")
    setPrimitiveValue(values["serves"], forKey:"serves")
    setPrimitiveValue(values["type"], forKey:"type")
    didChangeValueForKey("name")
    didChangeValueForKey("desc")
    didChangeValueForKey("serves")
    didChangeValueForKey("type")
}
```

In this example code, we're handling all the change notifications ourselves and setting the values into our NSManagedObject directly using the -setPrimitiveValue:forKey: method. This will cause all the values to be updated prior to the notifications being fired.

Accessing Relationships

Accessing relationships on an NSManagedObject is nearly as easy as accessing attributes. There's a tiny bit of a difference between working with a to-one relationship and a to-many relationship, though.

Accessing a To-One Relationship

When we're accessing a to-one relationship, we can treat it the same as we do an attribute. Because Core Data is first and foremost an object graph, a to-one relationship can be treated exactly like a property that contains any other object. For example, the relationship between RecipeIngredient and its Recipe is a to-one relationship from the RecipeIngredient side. So, if we were accessing this relationship from that point of view, the code would be as follows:

```
let ingredient = ...
let recipe = ingredient.valueForKey("recipe") as! NSManagedObject
```

In this example, we're using the -valueForKey: KVC method to access the relationship, and the NSManagedObject returns the object on the other side of the relationship, which is the entity. Likewise, to set the recipe for an ingredient, we'd use the following code:

```
let ingredient = ...
let recipe = ...
ingredient.setValue(recipe, forKey:"recipe")
```

This will set the object on the other side of the relationship.

Accessing a To-Many Relationship

The many side of a relationship is stored unordered. This means each time we fetch the objects on the many side of a relationship, the order isn't guaranteed, and it's likely that the order will change between fetches. However, we're guaranteed that each object will be included only once. In other words, when we access a to-many relationship using KVC, we'll get an NSSet back. For example, if we want to access the ingredients of a recipe, we'd use code similar to the following:

```
let recipe = ...
let ingredients = recipe.valueForKey("ingredients")
```

Likewise, setting the ingredients into a recipe is as follows:

```
let recipe = ...
let someIngredients = ...
recipe.setValue(someIngredients, forKey:"ingredients")
```

This will set which ingredients are associated with the recipe.

Mutable Access of To-Many Relationships

You might notice that the NSSet we get back when accessing a to-many relationship is immutable. Adding an object to a to-many relationship with an immutable NSSet requires creating a mutable copy of the NSSet, adding the new object to the NSMutableSet, and setting the NSMutableSet back onto the parent object. It's a painful process and, fortunately, unnecessary. When we want to add an object to a to-many relationship, we can use mutableSetValueForKey(:) in the place of valueForKey(:). This returns an NSMutableSet for us that's already associated with the parent object and reduces our code to the following:

```
let newIngredient = ...
let recipe = ...
let ingredients = recipe.mutableSetValueForKey("ingredients")
ingredients.addObject(newIngredient)
```

Note that we didn't need to set the NSMutableSet back into the entity, and therefore the code to add an object to a to-many relationship is quite short.

One important thing to notice in these relationship examples is that when we update the relationship, we're updating only one side of it. Because we defined these relationships as double-sided (that is, they include an inverse relationship that we defined in *Introducing the NSManagedObjectModel*, on page 15), Core Data handles keeping the integrity of the relationships intact. When we update one side of a relationship, Core Data automatically goes in and sets the other side for us.

Primitive Access

Similar to the process of accessing attributes discussed earlier, changes to a relationship will fire KVO notifications. Since there are situations in which we don't want this to occur or in which we want a finer-grained control over the notifications, there are primitive accessors for relationships as well. However, there's no primitive method for retrieving an NSMutableSet for a to-many relationship. Therefore, if the code requires changes to a relationship with either delayed or no observations being fired, we must use primitiveValueForKey(:) to get back an NSSet, assign it to a var, add our new object to the collection, and finally use setPrimitiveValue(:forKey:) to apply the changes.

Property Accessors

Relationships can use properties, just like the attributes discussed earlier. In the code in *Mutable Access of To-Many Relationships*, on page 24, if we want to add a property to retrieve the relationship, declare this property:

```
@NSManaged var recipeIngredients: [NSManagedObject]
```

Subclassing NSManagedObject

Although NSManagedObject provides a tremendous amount of flexibility and handles the majority of the work a data object normally does, it doesn't cover every possibility, and there are occasions where we might want to subclass it. Subclassing to gain @NSManaged (property) access to attributes and relationships is one common situation, but we may also want to add other convenience methods or additional functionality to the object. When such a situation arises, you must keep in mind some general rules.

Methods That Are Not Safe to Override

In Apple's documentation, the methods shown in this table should never be overridden.

primitiveValueForKey(:)	setPrimitiveValue(:forKey:)	isEqual(:)
hash()	superclass	class
self	zone	isProxy()
isKindOfClass(:)	isMemberOfClass(:)	conformsToProtocol(:)
respondsToSelector(:)	managedObjectContext()	entity
objectID	inserted	updated
deleted	fault	instancesRespondToSelector(:)
instanceMethodForSelector(:)	methodForSelector(:)	methodSignatureForSelector(:)
isSubclassOfClass(:)		

Table 1—Methods never to override

It's quite a list. Most, if not all, of these methods are common sense, and experience with Objective-C/Swift/Cocoa explains why they should not be overridden. Even though this is a fairly long list, I'm going to add a few more.

init

The first is init. There's really no reason or benefit to overriding the init methods of an NSManagedObject, and there are situations in which doing so has unpredictable results. Although it isn't specifically against the documentation to override the init methods, I recommend strongly against it. The awakeFromInsert() and awakeFromFetch() methods provide sufficient access that overriding init is unnecessary. (Both awakeFromInsert() and awakeFromFetch() are discussed in more depth later in this chapter.)

KVO Methods

I'd also add all of the KVO methods. The documentation flags these methods as "discouraged," but I'd put them right in the "do not subclass" list. There's no reason to override these methods, and any logic that you'd want to put into them can probably be put somewhere else with fewer issues.

description()

In addition, there's the description() method, used fairly often in logging. It's a great way to dump the contents of an object out to the logs during debugging. However, when we're dealing with faults (discussed in Chapter 5, *Performance Tuning*, on page 65), we don't want to fire a fault in the description() method. Since the default implementation of description() does the right thing with regard to faults, it's best that we not try to override its behavior.

 Joe asks:
What Is a Fault?

Core Data faults are similar to virtual memory page faults. Faulted objects are scoped objects that may or may not actually be in memory, or "realized," until you use them. Although there's no guarantee for when a faulted NSManagedObject will be loaded into memory, it's guaranteed to be loaded when accessed. However, the object will be an instance of the appropriate class (either an NSManagedObject or the designated subclass), but its attributes aren't initialized.

Methods to Override

With the long list of methods that we shouldn't override, what methods should we consider overriding? There are a few methods we'll commonly override.

didTurnIntoFault()

This method is called after the NSManagedObject has been turned into a fault. It's a good place to release transient resources. One important thing to note is that when this method is called, all the stored values/relationships in the NSManagedObject are already out of memory. If you access any of them, it will fire the fault and pull them all back into memory again.

willTurnIntoFault()

Similar to didTurnIntoFault(), this method is called just before the NSManagedObject is turned into a fault. If your code needs to access attributes or relationships on the NSManagedObject before it's turned into a fault, then this is the entry point to use. Transient resources that impact attributes and relationships should be released here.

awakeFromInsert()

As mentioned, overriding any of the init methods is risky and unnecessary. However, it's very useful to be able to prepare an NSManagedObject before it starts accepting data. Perhaps we want to set up some logical defaults or assign some relationships before handing the object to the user. In these situations, we use awakeFromInsert(). As the name implies, this method is called right after the NSManagedObject is created from an insert call. This method is called before any values are set and is a perfect opportunity to set default values, initialize transient properties, and perform other tasks that we'd normally handle in the -init method. This method is called exactly once in the entire lifetime of an object. It won't be called on the next execution of the application, and it won't be called when an object is read in from the persistent store. Therefore, we don't need to worry about overriding values that have been set previously. When we override this method, we should be sure to call super.awakeFromInsert() at the very beginning of our implementation to allow the NSManagedObject to finish anything it needs to before we begin our code.

awakeFromFetch()

awakeFromFetch() is the counterpart to awakeFromInsert(). The awakeFromFetch() method will be called every time the object is retrieved from the persistent store (that is, loaded from disk). This method is highly useful for setting up transient objects or connections that the NSManagedObject will use during its life cycle. At this point in the creation of the NSManagedObject, the observation of changes to the object (or other objects) is turned off, and Core Data won't be aware of any changes made. Ideally, we should avoid making any changes to relationships during this method because the inverse won't be set. However, if we explicitly set both sides of the relationship, it's possible to make changes here. Like the awakeFromInsert() method, when we override this method, we should call super.awakeFromFetch() before any of our own code is called.

Now that we've explored creating and accessing instances of NSManagedObject, let's look at how to retrieve them.

Building an NSFetchRequest

NSFetchRequest is the part of Core Data that causes people to think it's a database API instead of an object hierarchy. When we want to retrieve objects from Core Data, we normally use an NSFetchRequest to do the retrieval. It's best to view an NSFetchRequest as a way to retrieve *all* instances of an entity from the object hierarchy, with the option to filter the results with an NSPredicate. There are two parts to the creation of an NSFetchRequest: setting the entity to be retrieved and optionally defining an NSPredicate to filter the objects that we want retrieved.

Setting the Entity

One thing that we must do as part of every NSFetchRequest is define the entity we want returned from the fetch. We do this by passing the appropriate NSEntityDescription to the NSFetchRequest. For example, if we want to retrieve Recipe entities, we construct the NSFetchRequest as follows:

```
let request = NSFetchRequest(entityName: "Recipe")
```

In this example, we construct a new NSFetchRequest and pass it the string "Recipe", which will be resolved into the NSEntityDescription associated with that entity. We can also grab a reference to the NSEntityDescription directly instead of allowing the NSFetchRequest to resolve it:

```
let moc = self.managedObjectContext
let request = NSFetchRequest()
let entity = NSEntityDescription.entityForName("Recipe",
    inManagedObjectContext:moc)
```

The difference between these two initializers is one of timing. In the first example, the NSEntityDescription is resolved when the request is executed, and the second example resolves the entity immediately. If the fetch request is going to be used much later than when it's constructed, then the second version may be preferable. However, the first version is much cleaner and easier to consume.

Executing a Fetch Request

Once we've constructed our NSFetchRequest, we need to execute it against the NSManagedObjectContext to get the results. Like a result set when accessing a database, an executed NSFetchRequest will return a collection of entities matching our search criteria. Since it's possible that a search might fail, the execution of an NSFetchRequest is flagged with throws and therefore requires a try keyword and ideally a do/catch block. For example, if we want to execute the fetch from the previous example, we use the following code:

```
let moc = self.managedObjectContext
let request = NSFetchRequest(entityName: "Recipe")
let results: [NSManagedObject]? = nil
do {
  results = try moc.executeFetchRequest(request)
} catch {
  fatalError("Failed to perform fetch: \(error)")
}
```

In this example, we call executeFetchRequest(:) on the NSManagedObjectContext, passing in the NSFetchRequest inside of a do/catch block. If the fetch failed, the

NSError will describes the problem. In that situation, we dump the error via a call to fatalError. If there's no error, we can proceed with our code. Note that the collection is guaranteed to not be nil after the catch, but it could be empty if no results are returned.

NSPredicate

When we don't want every instance of an entity returned, we use an NSPredicate to narrow the search or filter the results. The NSPredicate class is quite complex and powerful and can be used for more things than just Core Data. It's frequently used to filter the results of collection classes by acting on the KVC API and doing logic checks on the objects contained in the collection. One of the most common ways to use an NSPredicate is to construct a SQL-like query, such as the following example:

```
let moc = self.managedObjectContext
let request = NSFetchRequest(entityName: "Recipe")
request.predicate = NSPredicate(format: "serves > 10", arguments: nil)
```

There are many different ways to build an NSPredicate. The one shown in the previous example accepts a SQL-like string and can accept any number of parameters after the string. For example, if we were going to pass in the number of servings, we'd rewrite the NSPredicate as follows:

```
let args = [10];
let moc = self.managedObjectContext
let request = NSFetchRequest(entityName: "Recipe")
let predicate = NSPredicate(format: "serves > %@", argumentArray:args)
request.predicate = predicate
```

It's possible to add as many parameters to the NSPredicate as needed. The NSPredicate class is quite flexible and can be used in a large number of ways. For further reading on how to use the class to its full potential, I recommend Apple's *Predicate Programming Guide.*[2]

Stored Fetch Requests

In addition to constructing the NSFetchRequest directly in code, it's possible to build them within the data model and store them for later use. By storing the fetch requests within the model itself, we can change them as needed without having to go through all the code looking for every place that they're used. Simply changing them in the model will automatically update them wherever they're being used. To store an NSFetchRequest within the data model, we select the entity that we want to run the request against and choose Design > Data

---

2.   http://developer.apple.com/documentation/Cocoa/Conceptual/Predicates/Articles/pUsing.html

Model > Add Fetch Request from the main menu. From there we'll be able to set the name of the fetch request and define its predicate, as shown here.

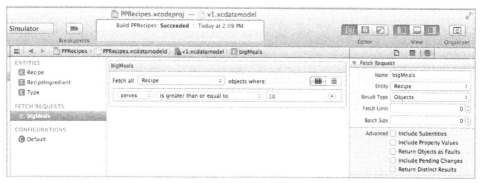

Once we have the fetch request in our data model, we can request a reference to it by asking the NSManagedObjectModel. Once we have a reference to the NSFetchRequest, we can execute it in the same manner as we do with an NSFetchRequest that has been constructed in code.

PPRecipes/PPRecipes/PPRSelectIngredientTypeViewController.swift

```swift
let moc = managedObjectContext!
let psc = moc.persistentStoreCoordinator!
let model = psc.managedObjectModel
let name = "allIngredients"
guard let request = model.fetchRequestTemplateForName(name) else {
  fatalError("Failed to find fetch request in the model")
}
request.sortDescriptors = [NSSortDescriptor(key: "name",
  ascending: true)]
```

As shown, we call the -fetchRequestTemplateForName: method on the NSManagedObjectModel, which returns a fully formed NSFetchRequest to us. This NSFetchRequest will already have the NSEntityDescription and NSPredicate set, so we can execute the NSFetchRequest immediately. We can also update this NSFetchRequest to include sort descriptors if needed.

NSSortDescriptor

NSSortDescriptor has been around longer than Core Data, and it's still quite useful for ordering data. As mentioned previously, data that comes from a to-many relationship is unordered by default, and it's up to us to order it. So, if we wanted to retrieve all the recipes and sort them by their name property in alphabetical order, we'd require another step as part of the fetch.

```swift
let fetch = NSFetchRequest(entityName: "Recipe")
fetch.sortDescriptors = [NSSortDescriptor(key: "name", ascending: true)]
```

> ## Fetched Properties
>
> In addition to NSFetchRequest objects, we have the ability to define a lazy relationship between objects. Fetched properties are kind of a cross between relationships and the NSFetchRequest. A fetched property isn't a relationship in the strictest sense and isn't realized until the property is requested. When the property is accessed, Core Data performs the underlying NSFetchRequest and returns the result. Unlike a normal relationship, a fetched property is returned as an NSArray as opposed to an NSSet.
>
> In practice, I've found fetched properties to be less useful and less flexible than either creating a stored fetch request or building the fetch request in code. Usually when a situation calls for a fetched property, it tends to be easier to subclass the entity in question, perform an NSFetchRequest in code, and return the results.

In this example, we are retrieving all the Recipe entities by creating an NSFetchRequest with the NSEntityDescription set to our entity and no predicate. However, in addition to fetching the Recipe entities, we want them sorted. We accomplish the sorting by adding a collection of NSSortDescriptor instances directly to the NSFetchRequest, which causes the returned collection to be properly sorted.

The NSSortDescriptor takes two parameters as part of its init: a key and a Bool denoting whether the sort is ascending or descending. We can have as many NSSortDescriptor objects as we want as part of the sort, and therefore they're placed within a collection prior to the sort being performed.

Adding an NSSortDescriptor is especially useful on Cocoa Touch because the NSFetchedResultsController continues to keep its results sorted without any intervention on our part. The NSFetchedResultsController is discussed in more depth in Chapter 3, *iOS: NSFetchedResultsController*, on page 33.

Wrapping Up

We covered a large number of the important pieces of Core Data in this chapter. We discussed what is part of the Core Data stack as well as what tools we have available to access the data maintained by Core Data. As we continue to explore Core Data in depth, please use this chapter as a reference point for the aspects of Core Data and how they all fit together. By the end of the book, each of these elements should be very familiar to you.

Now that you have a firm understanding of the primary objects within Core Data, we can explore how to best integrate Core Data with an iOS application.

CHAPTER 3

iOS: NSFetchedResultsController

The NSFetchedResultsController was introduced alongside Core Data when the framework was added to iOS with version 3.0. Since its introduction, developers have settled into a love–hate relationship with this class. When it's used in the way it was intended, it works extremely well. The hate part comes in when developers attempt to use the NSFetchedResultsController outside of its intended niche—that's when things start to fall apart quite quickly. The NSFetchedResultsController is designed to be the glue between Core Data and the UITableView. When Core Data was first added to iOS, the Core Data team realized that there was a significant amount of work to get Core Data and table views talking well. They removed nearly all of that work with the introduction of the NSFetchedResultsController. In this chapter, we will talk about what the NSFetchedResultsController is designed to do and how it works. Once you have a handle on how it works, we'll explore alternatives so you know what to use when NSFetchedResultsController isn't the correct fit.

How to Use the NSFetchedResultsController

When Core Data was added to iOS, it was clear to the Core Data team that Core Data and the UITableView would be used together extensively. They also realized that getting these two pieces to work together smoothly would require a fair amount of code that could be abstracted away; that abstraction is the NSFetchedResultsController. The NSFetchedResultsController is the glue that binds a UITableView to Core Data so that we need to write very little code.

The purpose of the NSFetchedResultsController is twofold. The NSFetchedResultsController is designed to retrieve data from Core Data and store that data for access. It does this with an internal NSFetchRequest that it uses for the retrieval. It then stores the data and makes it available for use. As part of the storage and retrieval, the NSFetchedResultsController organizes the returned data into sections, in the process making the data more useful to a UITableView.

The NSFetchedResultsController's second purpose is to monitor changes in the data. Without having the ability to be notified when the data has changed, the NSFetchedResultsController wouldn't be much more use than an NSArray. When the NSManagedObjectContext associated with the NSFetchedResultsController changes, the NSFetchedResultsController checks to see whether any of the objects it's referencing are impacted. Further, it also watches inserts to determine whether any newly inserted objects should be included in what's being referenced. If any changes occur, the NSFetchedResultsController notifies its delegate of the changes. The delegate is normally its associated UITableView.

Standing Up an NSFetchedResultsController

The creation of a NSFetchedResultsController takes a number of steps and uses several of the classes that we discussed in Chapter 2, *Under the Hood*, on page 13.

PPRecipes/PPRecipes/PPRMasterViewController.swift

```swift
let fetch = NSFetchRequest(entityName: "Recipe")
fetch.sortDescriptors = [NSSortDescriptor(key: "name", ascending: true)]

guard let moc = managedObjectContext else {
  fatalError("MOC not initialized")
}
fResultsController = NSFetchedResultsController(fetchRequest: fetch,
  managedObjectContext: moc, sectionNameKeyPath: nil, cacheName: nil)
fResultsController?.delegate = self
do {
  try fResultsController?.performFetch()
} catch {
  fatalError("Unable to fetch: \(error)")
}
```

The NSFetchedResultsController is effectively a wrapper around an NSFetchRequest. Therefore, we first need to construct the NSFetchRequest that will be used. In this example, we're building an NSFetchRequest that retrieves all the available recipes. Further, we're going to sort the Recipe entities based on their name attribute. Once we have built the NSFetchRequest, we then construct the NSFetchedResultsController. In its initialization, it accepts an NSFetchRequest, an NSManagedObjectContext, a string for its sectionNameKeyPath, and another string for its cacheName. Let's explore each of these in turn.

NSFetchRequest

The NSFetchRequest retrieves the data from Core Data and makes it available for use. This is the NSFetchRequest we just defined in code.

NSManagedObjectContext

The NSFetchedResultsController requires an NSManagedObjectContext to perform the fetch against. Additionally, the NSManagedObjectContext that the NSFetchedResultsController will be monitoring for changes. Note that the NSFetchedResultsController is designed to work against user interface elements, and therefore, it works best when it's pointed at an NSManagedObjectContext that's running on the main/UI thread. Threading is discussed in more depth in Chapter 6, *Threading*, on page 79.

sectionNameKeyPath

The NSFetchedResultsController uses the sectionNameKeyPath to break the retrieved data into sections. Once the data is retrieved, the NSFetchedResultsController calls for a property on each entity using KVC (more on this in Chapter 11, *Bindings, KVC, and KVO*, on page 157). The value of that property will be used to break the data into sections. In our current example, we have this set to nil, which means our data won't be broken into sections. We can easily add it, as follows:

PPRecipes/PPRecipes/PPRMasterViewController.swift

```
let fetch = NSFetchRequest(entityName: "Recipe")
fetch.sortDescriptors = [NSSortDescriptor(key: "type", ascending: true),
  NSSortDescriptor(key: "name", ascending: true)]

guard let moc = managedObjectContext else {
  fatalError("MOC not initialized")
}
fResultsController = NSFetchedResultsController(fetchRequest: fetch,
  managedObjectContext: moc, sectionNameKeyPath: "type",
  cacheName: "Master")
fResultsController?.delegate = self
do {
  try fResultsController?.performFetch()
} catch {
  fatalError("Unable to fetch: \(error)")
}
```

Something to note here is that along with passing in "type" to the initialization of the NSFetchedResultsController, we also added a second NSSortDescriptor to the NSFetchRequest. The NSFetchedResultsController requires the data to be returned in the same order as it will appear in the sections. As a result, we must sort the data first by type and then by name.

cacheName

The last property of the initialization of the NSFetchedResultsController is the
cacheName. This value is used by the NSFetchedResultsController to build up a small
data cache on disk. That cache will allow the NSFetchedResultsController to skip
the NSPersistentStore entirely when its associated UITableView is reconstructed.
This cache can dramatically improve the launch performance of any associated
UITableView. However, this cache is extremely sensitive to changes in the data
and the NSFetchRequest. Therefore, this cache name can't be reused from one
UITableView to another, nor can it be reused if the NSPredicate changes.

Once the NSFetchedResultsController has been initialized, we need to populate it
with data. This can be done immediately upon initialization, as in our current
example, or it can be done later. When to populate the NSFetchedResultsController
is more of a performance question. If the associated UITableView is constructed
very early, we may want to wait to populate the NSFetchedResultsController until
the UITableView is about to be used. For now and until we can determine if
there's a performance issue, we'll populate it upon initialization. This is done
with a call to performFetch(), which can throw so therefore is wrapped in a
do/catch block. If there's an error in the fetch, the catch block (which we
have just throwing a fatalError) will be executed.

Wiring the NSFetchedResultsController to a UITableView

Now that we have our NSFetchedResultsController initialized, we need to wire it into
its associated UITableView. We do this within the various UITableViewDatasource
methods. At a minimum, we need to implement two of them, but implementing
the core three is better.

PPRecipes/PPRecipes/PPRMasterViewController.swift

```
override func numberOfSectionsInTableView(tableView: UITableView) -> Int {
  guard let count = fResultsController?.sections?.count else {
    fatalError("Failed to resolve FRC")
  }
  return count
}
```

The first one is numberOfSectionsInTableView(). Here we ask the NSFetchedResultsController
to return its array of sections, and we return the count of them. If we don't
have a sectionNameKeyPath set on the NSFetchedResultsController, there will be either
zero or one section in that array. In previous versions of iOS (prior to iOS 4.*x*),
the UITableView did not like being told there were zero sections. You may run
across older code that checks the section count and always returns a minimum

of one section (with zero rows). That issue has been addressed, and the associated check is no longer needed.

PPRecipes/PPRecipes/PPRMasterViewController.swift

```swift
override func tableView(tableView: UITableView,
  numberOfRowsInSection section: Int) -> Int {
  guard let sectionInfo = fResultsController?.sections?[section] else {
    fatalError("Failed to resolve FRC")
  }
  return sectionInfo.numberOfObjects
}
```

The tableView(: numberOfRowsInSection:) method is slightly more complex. Here, we grab the array of sections, but we also grab the object within the array that's at the index being passed into the method. There's no need to check to see whether the index is valid since the numberOfSectionsInTableView() method is the basis for this index. The object that's in the array is undetermined but guaranteed to respond to the NSFetchedResultsSectionInfo protocol. One of the methods on that protocol is numberOfObjects, which we use to return the number of rows in the section.

PPRecipes/PPRecipes/PPRMasterViewController.swift

```swift
override func tableView(tableView: UITableView,
  cellForRowAtIndexPath indexPath: NSIndexPath) -> UITableViewCell {
  guard let frc = fResultsController else {
    fatalError("Failed to resolve NSFetchedResultsController")
  }
  guard let obj = frc.objectAtIndexPath(indexPath) as? NSManagedObject else {
    fatalError("Failed to resolve NSManagedObject")
  }
  guard let cell = tableView.dequeueReusableCellWithIdentifier("Cell") else {
    fatalError("Failed to dequeue cell")
  }
  cell.textLabel?.text = obj.valueForKey("name") as? String
  return cell
}
```

In the tableView(: cellForRowAtIndexPath:) method, we use another useful ability of the NSFetchedResultsController: the objectAtIndexPath() method. With this method, we can retrieve the exact object we need to work with in a single call. This reduces the complexity of our tableView(: cellForRowAtIndexPath:) method significantly.

There are many additional examples of how to wire in the NSFetchedResultsController to the UITableView, but these three highlight the most common usage. Even with just these three methods, you can see how the NSFetchedResultsController drastically reduces the amount of code you need to write (and thereby maintain) to access the data to be displayed.

Listening to the NSFetchedResultsController

In addition to making it easy for us to retrieve and display the data for a UITableView, the NSFetchedResultsController makes it relatively painless to handle changes in that data. If the values within one of our recipes changes (perhaps through iCloud, as discussed in Chapter 9, *Using Core Data with iCloud*, on page 123, or through an import), we want our UITableView to immediately reflect those changes. In addition, if a recipe is removed or added, we want our UITableView to be accurate. To make sure these updates happen, we must add the delegate methods for the NSFetchedResultsControllerDelegate protocol. It's common for the UIViewController to also be the delegate for the NSFetchedResultsController. There are five methods in this protocol; let's look at each of them.

controllerWillChangeContent()

The first method, controllerWillChangeContent(), tells us that changes are about to start. This method is our opportunity to instruct the UITableView that changes are coming. Typically this is where we tell the UITableView to stop updating the user interface so that all of the changes can be displayed at once.

PPRecipes/PPRecipes/PPRMasterViewController.swift

```
func controllerWillChangeContent(controller: NSFetchedResultsController) {
  tableView.beginUpdates()
}
```

controller(: didChangeSection: atIndex: forChangeType:)

This method is called when a section changes. The only valid change types are NSFetchedResultsChangeInsert and NSFetchedResultsChangeDelete. This is our opportunity to tell the UITableView that a section is being added or removed.

PPRecipes/PPRecipes/PPRMasterViewController.swift

```
func controller(controller: NSFetchedResultsController,
  didChangeSection sectionInfo: NSFetchedResultsSectionInfo,
  atIndex sectionIndex: Int,
      forChangeType type: NSFetchedResultsChangeType) {
  switch type {
  case .Insert:
    tableView.insertSections(NSIndexSet(index: sectionIndex),
      withRowAnimation: .Fade)
  case .Delete:
    tableView.deleteSections(NSIndexSet(index: sectionIndex),
      withRowAnimation: .Fade)
  case .Move: break
  case .Update: break
  }
}
```

Here we use a switch to determine what the change type is and pass it along to the UITableView. You may note that there are two case statements at the end of this that don't react. They're added to satisfy the compiler and at this time aren't being used in this method.

controller(: didChangeObject: atIndexPath: forChangeType: newIndexPath:)

This is the most complex method in the NSFetchedResultsControllerDelegate protocol. In this method, we're notified of any changes to any data object. There are four types of changes that we need to react to, listed next.

PPRecipes/PPRecipes/PPRMasterViewController.swift

```
func controller(controller: NSFetchedResultsController,
  didChangeObject anObject: AnyObject, atIndexPath indexPath: NSIndexPath?,
  forChangeType type: NSFetchedResultsChangeType,
  newIndexPath: NSIndexPath?) {
  switch type {
  case .Insert:
    guard let nip = newIndexPath else { fatalError("How?") }
    tableView.insertRowsAtIndexPaths([nip!], withRowAnimation: .Fade)
  case .Delete:
    guard let ip = indexPath else { fatalError("How?") }
    tableView.deleteRowsAtIndexPaths([ip!], withRowAnimation: .Fade)
  case .Move:
    guard let nip = newIndexPath else { fatalError("How?") }
    guard let ip = indexPath else { fatalError("How?") }
    tableView.deleteRowsAtIndexPaths([ip!], withRowAnimation: .Fade)
    tableView.insertRowsAtIndexPaths([nip!], withRowAnimation: .Fade)
  case .Update:
    guard let ip = indexPath else { fatalError("How?") }
    tableView.reloadRowsAtIndexPaths([ip!], withRowAnimation: .Fade)
  }
}
```

An NSFetchedResultsChangeInsert is fired when a new object is inserted that we need to display in our UITableView. When we receive this call, we pass it along to the UITableView and tell the table view what type of animation to use.

An NSFetchedResultsChangeDelete is fired when an existing object is removed. Just as we do with an insert, we pass this information along to the UITableView and tell it what type of animation to use when removing the row.

An NSFetchedResultsChangeUpdate is fired when an existing object has changed internally—in other words, when one of its attributes has been updated. We don't know from this call if it's an attribute that we care about. Instead of spending time determining whether we *should* update the row, it's generally cheaper to just update the row.

An NSFetchedResultsChangeMove is fired when a row is moved. The move could be as a result of a number of factors but is generally caused by a data change resulting in the row being displayed in a different location. In our example, if the name or type of a recipe were altered, it'd most likely cause this change type. It's quite possible—and common—to receive an NSFetchedResultsChangeMove and an NSFetchedResultsChangeUpdate in the same batch of changes. When this change type is received, we make two calls to the UITableView: one to remove the row from its previous location and another to insert it into its new location.

controller(: sectionIndexTitleForSectionName:)

We use this method when we want to massage the data coming back from our NSFetchedResultsController before it's passed to the UITableView for display. One situation where this might be necessary is if we want to remove any extended characters from the title before it's displayed; another example is if we want to add something to the displayed title that isn't in the data.

PPRecipes/PPRecipes/PPRMasterViewController.swift

```
func controller(controller: NSFetchedResultsController,
  sectionIndexTitleForSectionName sectionName: String) -> String? {
  return "[\(sectionName)]"
}
```

controllerDidChangeContent()

The final method tells us that this round of changes is finished and we can tell the UITableView to update the user interface. We can also use this method to update any other parts of the user interface outside of the UITableView. For example, if we had a count of the number of recipes displayed, we'd update that count here.

PPRecipes/PPRecipes/PPRMasterViewController.swift

```
func controllerDidChangeContent(controller: NSFetchedResultsController) {
  tableView.endUpdates()
}
```

With the implementation of the five methods described, our UITableView can now retrieve, display, and update its display without any further work from us. In fact, a large portion of the code in the NSFetchedResultsControllerDelegate methods is fairly boilerplate and can be moved from project to project, further reducing the amount of "new" code we need to maintain.

Under the Hood of the NSFetchedResultsController

We can see the value of an NSFetchedResultsController, but how does it actually work? When I started to explore the details, I was shocked to find out that I could duplicate much of the behavior of the NSFetchedResultsController using publicly available APIs.

This means that, instead of trying to cram the NSFetchedResultsController into places that it almost fits (or worse), you can build your own that behaves exactly in the way that you need to. By using publicly exposed APIs, the Core Data team has invited us to build our own observers of Core Data so that non–table view user interfaces can react to changes in the data easily.

At its core, the NSFetchedResultsController takes advantage of the notifications that an NSManagedObjectContext fires off. When we initialize the NSFetchedResultsController, it sets itself up as an observer and then reacts as the notifications come in.

NSManagedObjectContextObjectsDidChangeNotification

One of the three notifications that the NSFetchedResultsController listens for is the NSManagedObjectContextObjectsDidChangeNotification. This very chatty notification tells the NSFetchedResultsController whenever one of the attributes of any object has changed. The NSFetchedResultsController uses this information, combined with its NSFetchRequest, to determine whether it needs to notify its delegate of the changes. These changes often result in a call to controller(: didChangeObject: atIndexPath: forChangeType: newIndexPath:), with a change type of NSFetchedResultsChangeUpdate and/or NSFetchedResultsChangeMove.

NSManagedObjectContextWillSaveNotification

Without access to the source code of the NSFetchedResultsController, I can't say with 100 percent certainty that this notification is used; however, it appears that NSManagedObjectContextWillSaveNotification is being used to catch when an object is deleted. When an object is deleted, the NSFetchedResultsController determines whether it's relevant to our NSFetchRequest and issues the appropriate delegate callbacks. This would typically result in a call to controller(: didChangeSection: atIndex: forChangeType:) if the deletion caused a section to disappear and/or a call to the controller(: didChangeObject: atIndexPath: forChangeType: newIndexPath:) with a change type of NSFetchedResultsChangeDelete.

NSManagedObjectContextDidSaveNotification

The final NSNotification type is fired after the NSManagedObjectContext has completed its save. This notification is observed so that the NSFetchedResultsController can capture any objects that are newly inserted or have been changed in another context and propagated (as discussed in Chapter 6, *Threading*, on page 79). This would typically result in a call to controller(: didChangeSection: atIndex: forChangeType:) if the insertion/update caused a section to disappear or appear.

It would also cause a call to controller(: didChangeObject: atIndexPath: forChangeType: newIndexPath:) with any of the change types available.

Beyond listening for these notifications, the NSFetchedResultsController is just a container. The cache is likely a serialization of the currently fetched objects (although I haven't been able to figure out its exact data structure yet).

Why is this information valuable? For one, it's always helpful to understand how things work so that when they stop working, we can investigate them and resolve the issue. In addition, since the NSFetchedResultsController has such an extremely narrow focus, we don't want to use it in situations where we don't have a UITableView to populate. However, it's so useful that we really want to use some of its features outside of this narrow focus. With an understanding of how it works comes the ability to duplicate the features that are useful.

Building Our Own: MSZContextWatcher

Since the introduction of the NSFetchedResultsController, I've run into numerous situations in which I wanted to use its ability to detect data changes even when I wasn't using a UITableView. Building a user interface for an iPad where three different entities are being displayed at once is a situation that begs for some kind of watcher to notify the user interface when the data has changed. Needing to watch not just a single type of entity but also relationships associated with that entity is another place where an observer is useful. Frequently I'd attempt to use an NSFetchedResultsController and run into one problem or another that made it more difficult than it needed to be. This led me to investigate how the NSFetchedResultsController worked and finally resulted in the creation of the MSZContextWatcher.

The MSZContextWatcher is publicly available under the BSD license, and the most recent version is always stored in my public GitHub repository at http://github.com/mzarra/MSZ_Shared.

The goal of the MSZContextWatcher is to provide us with the ability to monitor a subset of the data that's in Core Data and to be notified when it changes. It's the same functionality that's in the NSFetchedResultsController but not as tightly coupled with the UITableView.

The API to use this class is composed of an initializer and two methods.

init()

We initialize the MSZContextWatcher with an NSManagedObjectContext. This NSManagedObjectContext is used when it sets itself up as an observer on NSNotificationCenter. This avoids notifications coming from other NSManagedObjectContext instances.

PPRecipes/PPRecipes/MSZContextWatcher.swift

```
init(context: NSManagedObjectContext) {
  guard let psc = context.persistentStoreCoordinator else {
    fatalError("No PSC in context")
  }
  persistentStoreCoordinator = psc

  super.init()

  let center = NSNotificationCenter.defaultCenter()
  center.addObserver(self, selector: #selector(contextUpdated(_:)),
    name: NSManagedObjectContextDidSaveNotification, object: nil)
}
```

addEntityToWatch(: withPredicate:)

The second method in the public API for the MSZContextWatcher allows us to define what the watcher is listening for. This is moved away from the initialization because I wanted the ability to watch more than one entity and/or more than one predicate. With this method, I can add as many entities and/or predicates as I need.

PPRecipes/PPRecipes/MSZContextWatcher.swift

```
func addEntityToWatch(desc: NSEntityDescription, predicate: NSPredicate) {
  guard let name = desc.name else { fatalError("bad desc") }
  let entityPredicate = NSPredicate(format: "entity.name == %@", name)

  var array = [entityPredicate, predicate]
  let final = NSCompoundPredicate(andPredicateWithSubpredicates: array)

  if masterPredicate == nil {
    masterPredicate = final
    return
  }
  array = [masterPredicate!, final]
  masterPredicate = NSCompoundPredicate(orPredicateWithSubpredicates: array)
}
```

We do a bit of NSPredicate construction in the implementation. First, we take the passed-in NSEntityDescription and use that inside a new predicate that compares the entity name. Next, we create a compound predicate that combines the passed-in predicate with the new entity predicate with an AND join. Now we have a new predicate that checks to make sure the compared object is the same entity before we use the second part of the predicate against the object.

Why do we do this? If we just run the passed-in predicate against every object, we'll get an error when it hits an object that doesn't have one of the properties in the predicate. By adding a prefix predicate that checks the name of the entity, we're ensuring it will run only against the correct entity.

If there's no existing predicate in our MSZContextWatcher, we set our new compound predicate as the masterPredicate and return. However, if there's already a masterPredicate set, we need to compound the existing predicate with our new one. Again, we use an NSCompoundPredicate to combine the existing masterPredicate and our new predicate. However, this time we use an OR instead of an AND in the compound predicate. Finally, we take the newly created compound predicate and set that as the masterPredicate.

contextUpdated()

We've constructed a predicate that we can run against a collection of NSManagedObject instances, and it will filter out any objects that we don't care about. Now when we receive a notification from an NSManagedObjectContextDidSaveNotification, we can easily filter the incoming objects against our predicate.

PPRecipes/PPRecipes/MSZContextWatcher.swift

```swift
func contextUpdated(notification: NSNotification) {
  guard let predicate = masterPredicate else {
    fatalError("Master Predicate is not set")
  }
  guard let iContext = notification.object as? NSManagedObjectContext else {
    fatalError("Unexpected object in notification")
  }
  guard let iCoordinator = iContext.persistentStoreCoordinator else {
    fatalError("Incoming context has no PSC")
  }
  if iCoordinator != persistentStoreCoordinator { return }
  let info = notification.userInfo
  var results = [String:[NSManagedObject]]()
  var totalCount = 0
  if let insert = info?[NSInsertedObjectsKey] as? [NSManagedObject] {
    let filter = insert.filter{ return predicate.evaluateWithObject($0) }
    totalCount += filter.count
    results[NSInsertedObjectsKey] = filter
  }
  if let update = info?[NSUpdatedObjectsKey] as? [NSManagedObject] {
    let filter = update.filter{ return predicate.evaluateWithObject($0) }
    totalCount += filter.count
    results[NSUpdatedObjectsKey] = filter
  }
  if let delete = info?[NSDeletedObjectsKey] as? [NSManagedObject] {
    let filter = delete.filter{ return predicate.evaluateWithObject($0) }
    totalCount += filter.count
    results[NSDeletedObjectsKey] = filter
  }
  if totalCount == 0 { return }
  delegate?.contextUpdated(results)
}
```

When we receive a notification, we need to check the userInfo and see whether there are any objects that we care about. In the userInfo, there are up to three collections: one for updated objects, one for deleted objects, and one for inserted objects. We walk through each of these sets, grabbing a reference to each one, filtering the collection against our masterPredicate, and keeping track of how many objects are left. If no objects are left at the end of the filtering, we know there were none in the save that we cared about, and we can return.

If there were any objects left, we need to notify our delegate of them. Since we've already filtered the objects, we may as well pass them to our delegate so our delegate doesn't need to repeat the work. We create a new dictionary and add each of our collections to it using the same keys that the incoming NSNotification used. Once it's constructed, we can pass the newly created dictionary off to our delegate.

Now we have a class that allows us to watch any NSManagedObjectContext of our choosing and notifies us if an object that we care about has been touched in any way. We can make the predicate as broad or narrow as we want. By allowing the delegate to pass in the predicate, we've also made this class highly reusable.

Wrapping Up

The NSFetchedResultsController is a great time-saver when we're working with a UITableView. It can drastically reduce the amount of code we need to write and make our UITableView instances perform very well. However, it has a narrowly focused purpose, and it should be avoided when you're not working with a UITableView. Fortunately, with a little bit of effort, we can duplicate quite a bit of its functionality and create a highly flexible class that fits into a variety of situations.

CHAPTER 4

Versioning and Migration

Just like a battle plan, no codebase ever survives contact with users. As soon as users start to use an application, they want to change it. Even if the code is just for ourselves, we, also as users, will want to change things. For example, we may need to add an attribute or a new object and then restructure things to accommodate those changes. Additions and changes can be quite involved and invariably require a change in how the data is stored.

Starting with Mac OS X 10.5 Leopard and iOS 3.0, Apple has made data migration nearly trivial for users of Core Data. Taking the project outlined in Chapter 1, *Before We Begin*, on page 1, we'll add some additional features to it in succeeding versions. Although a data migration works even when there's no data stored, it's more useful to have some data to work with. Therefore, if you haven't added any recipes yet, I recommend you do so before we proceed.

In version 2, we'll add the ability to tag an author to a recipe as well as tag a "last used" date. That way, we know who created the delicious dish as well as the last time we made it. We certainly wouldn't want to accidentally make the same dish two days in a row!

In version 3, we'll normalize the repository a bit by extracting the ingredients and forming a many-to-many relationship back to the recipes. In addition, we'll add the concept of a shopping list to make it easier to ensure we pick up all the ingredients on our next trip to the store. Next, we'll extract the unitOfMeasure attribute from the RecipeIngredient entity into its own entity and allow that new entity to be linked to the new ingredient entity. This step gives us one lookup list for the various units of measure and reduces the risk of human error. Lastly, we'll remove the Meat and Fish entries from the Type attribute of the Recipe entity. Any recipe entries that are flagged with Meat or Fish will be updated to Entrée instead.

Some Maintenance Before We Migrate

Before we actually release a new version of our application that migrates the data, we need to first complete a minor "maintenance" update for our users. Normally, we'd add this code to the very first version of our application, but just in case we wrote that first release before versioning was a consideration, we need to go back to our old version and add a small amount of code to help our users.

Some users will download the new version of an application to just "try it out" and see if it's worth the upgrade price and the hassle. Normally this isn't an issue—until we upgrade the data underneath our users. Then things go sideways. What we *do not* want to happen is the error message shown here.

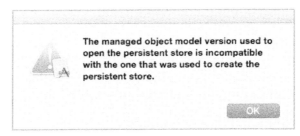

Note that this is the error message we'd see on OS X. On iOS, our application would simply crash on launch. This is a terrible user experience and something we want to avoid. Fortunately, the way to avoid it is very easy, and we can add it to a point release of our application before we do any migration. That way, when the users open the first version of our application after "testing" the second version, they get a friendly error message. Or we can take it a step further and restore/access the older version of their data.

PPRecipesV3/PPRecipes/AppDelegate.swift

```swift
func displayError(error: NSError) {
  var message = "The recipes database is either corrupt or was created by a"
  message += " newer version of Grokking Recipes. Please contact support to"
  message += " assist with this error. \n\(error.localizedDescription)"
  let alert = UIAlertController(title: "Error", message: message,
    preferredStyle: .Alert)
  let close = UIAlertAction(title: "Close", style: .Cancel, handler: {
    (action) in
    //Probably terminate the application
  })
  alert.addAction(close)
  if let controller = window?.rootViewController {
    controller.presentViewController(alert, animated: true, completion: nil)
  }
}
```

This function is designed to accept an NSError object and display an alert to the user.

The trigger for this function lies in the instantiation of the DataController. In the init() of the DataController, a closure was previously passed in with no parameters. In this version we add the acceptance of a NSError parameter that can be nil. When the closure is called, the application delegate checks to see if the error is in fact nil and, if it is, the application launch proceeds as normal. If, however, the error is *not* nil, then an error has occurred that needs to be displayed to the user.

PPRecipesV3/PPRecipes/AppDelegate.swift

```swift
func application(application: UIApplication, didFinishLaunchingWithOptions
  launchOptions: [NSObject: AnyObject]?) -> Bool {
  dataController = PPRDataController() {
    (inError) in
    if let error = inError {
      self.displayError(error)
    } else {
      self.contextInitialized()
    }
  }
}
```

With this change we can then alter the initializeCoreDataStack method to propagate the error.

PPRecipesV3/PPRecipes/PPRDataController.swift

```swift
do {
  try psc.addPersistentStoreWithType(NSSQLiteStoreType,
    configuration: nil, URL: storeURL, options: nil)
} catch let error as NSError {
  assertionFailure("Failed to add persistent store: \(error)")
  self.initializationComplete?(error)
}
```

In this change, instead of producing a fatalError() in the catch block, we send the error back through the closure to the AppDelegate for display to the user. The AppDelegate is then responsible for displaying the error and deciding the next course of action. Depending on the user experience and business decisions involved, it may make sense to simply quit the application or offer users the option to reset their data. Note that we also have an assertionFailure() before the call to the closure. When we're developing this application, we want to make *very* sure that a developer-level error fires here to avoid the risk of the user ever encountering it.

A Simple Migration

To demonstrate a simple migration, let's add the ability to attribute recipes to authors. To begin the versioning, the first thing we have to do is create a new managed object model (MOM) based on the first one. To do that, we select the existing model in Xcode and then choose Design > Data Model > Add Model Version.

Your First Data Model Version

When you first set up versioning, be sure to look inside the target in Xcode and update the Compile Sources section. If you don't see the .xcdatamodeld file inside the target, remove the xcdatamodel references from it and drag the entire xcdatamodeld bundle into the target. Otherwise, your application may complain about being unable to merge entities because it will treat each version of the model as an independent model.

Once this change has been completed, it's best to clean the project (delete any previously compiled code) by choosing Product > Clean from the main menu.

Creating a Versioned Data Model

This is the first time we've added a model version, so Xcode is going to create a new bundle for us called PPRecipes.xcdatamodeld and put the original MOM inside the bundle along with a new copy of the original MOM. To make things clearer in the example project, I renamed these MOM objects to v1.xcdatamodel and v2.xcdatamodel. Next, we need to select the PPRecipes.xcdatamodeld file and open the File Inspector Utility View (⌘ ⌥ 1). In the utility view, you'll see a Versioned Core Data Model section. (The Xcode templates have been bouncing back and forth on this issue over the past few versions. It's possible, depending on when you created your project, that you already have a versioned data model.) Inside that section is a Current option, allowing us to select which model file is the current one. Make sure it references v2, as shown here.

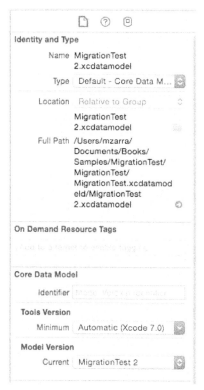

Now that we have a new version of the MOM, it's time to add the new entities and attributes. This process requires the addition of a new entity and some changes to the Recipe entity. Comparing the v1 data model and the v2 data model (as shown in the following figure on page 52), you can see that we added a new Author entity along with its one-to-many relationship with the Recipe entity. Also, the Recipe entity has a new attribute called lastUsed, which is defined as a Date.

We're not quite done. If we were to run the application right now, we'd trip the error that we discussed in *Some Maintenance Before We Migrate*, on page 48. Clearly, something is missing.

Version 1

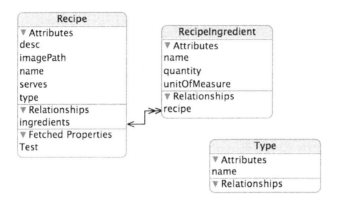

Version 2

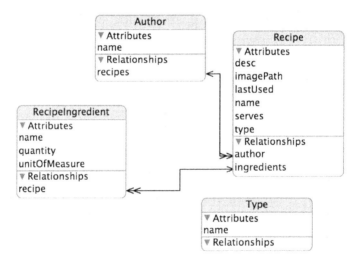

Turning On Automatic Data Migration

The first thing we need to do is to tell Core Data to automatically migrate data when the persistent store isn't using the same model as the current version. To do this, we need to make a small change to the persistentStoreCoordinator method in our PPRDataController. Previously we were passing nil to the addPersistentStoreWithType:configuration:URL:options:error: method for the options parameter. However, we must change that to the following:

PPRecipesV3/PPRecipes/PPRDataController.swift

```
let queue = dispatch_get_global_queue(DISPATCH_QUEUE_PRIORITY_DEFAULT, 0)
dispatch_async(queue) {
  let fileManager = NSFileManager.defaultManager()
  guard let documentsURL = fileManager.URLsForDirectory(.DocumentDirectory,
    inDomains: .UserDomainMask).first else {
    fatalError("Failed to resolve documents directory")
  }
  let storeURL = documentsURL.URLByAppendingPathComponent("PPRecipes.sqlite")

  do {
    let options = [NSMigratePersistentStoresAutomaticallyOption: true,
      NSInferMappingModelAutomaticallyOption: true]
    try psc.addPersistentStoreWithType(NSSQLiteStoreType,
      configuration: nil, URL: storeURL, options: options)
  } catch let error as NSError {
    assertionFailure("Failed to add persistent store: \(error)")
    self.initializationComplete?(error)
  }
```

The first of these options, NSMigratePersistentStoresAutomaticallyOption, tells Core Data to attempt a migration automatically if it determines that one is needed.

The second option, NSInferMappingModelAutomaticallyOption, instructs Core Data to resolve the mapping between the persistent store and the current model. If Core Data can figure this out, it will perform the migration.

For this migration, Core Data can easily resolve the changes that need to be made and will be able to do an inferred (automatic) migration for us. When the changes are more severe, we need to do a heavy, manual migration, as discussed in *A Heavy/Manual Migration*, on page 54.

With those changes made, we can run our application, and Core Data automatically handles the migration for us and updates the persistent store to the new model.

The Difference Between Light and Heavy Migrations

There are two types of migrations for Core Data: light (also referred to as lightweight or inferred) migration and heavy (also referred to as manual) migration. When we're working with SQLite persistent stores, the difference between these two types of migration is significant.

A light migration of a SQLite persistent store occurs within the SQLite file itself. No objects are loaded into memory, and therefore the memory requirements of the migration are quite low. In addition, since the migration is occurring within the database file, it's very fast. Although the size of the database file still affects the speed of the migration, a light migration of large database will still be remarkably faster than a heavy migration of a small database.

The speed and memory differences are so large that I recommend avoiding heavy migrations at nearly any cost.

A heavy migration is far more complicated than a light migration. When we perform a heavy migration, we must load each entity into memory, translate it from the old store to the new store, and then write it back out to disk. This requires two Core Data "stacks" in memory at the same time and a large amount of data processing in our application. It takes time—a lot of time. When a heavy migration is required, the application normally needs to show a wait dialog to the user so that the user knows what's going on.

In addition to the computational time, a heavy migration requires more work from the developer. When we're performing a light migration, we pass two options to Core Data and let the framework do the work. When we perform a heavy migration, we must explain the migration to Core Data. This requires us to create a mapping model, configure each entity in the mapping model, and sometimes even write code specific to a migration. As a result, there's a significant maintenance cost for the developer on top of the computational cost. All the same, it's a situation that may arise, so let's take a look at a heavy migration.

A Heavy/Manual Migration

A heavy migration is required when we go outside of the bounds of what a light migration can accomplish. A simple example of something that goes beyond a light migration is a *logic-based migration*. Imagine a situation in which, as part of a migration/application update, we need to change the data that's in the database. Perhaps there's a typo in the included data or a change in the logic. Changing the data during the migration is outside the scope of a light migration. However, we can easily add it to a heavy migration.

A more complex example would be a situation that involves normalizing data. In our application, each recipe has one or more recipe ingredients. If we wanted to expand our application and extract the common parts of the recipe ingredient into new tables, we'd be stepping outside the boundaries of what a light migration can accomplish.

In this migration, we're going to accomplish two goals. First we'll massage the data during the migration and find every occurrence of Meat or Fish for the recipe type and replace it with Entrée. In addition, we'll create new entities:

Ingredient and UnitOfMeasure. During the migration of the RecipeIngredient entity, we're going to create or associate the appropriate Ingredient to the RecipeIngredient.

Creating Our First Mapping Model

The first step is to create a mapping model for this migration. A *mapping model* is a description of how the migration is supposed to work. First we create a new file in Xcode, and select the section for Core Data. In that section is a template called Mapping Model, as shown here. Once we select that template, Xcode asks us to choose the data model version to use as the source. For this migration, we're going from v2 to v3, so we select v2. Then Xcode asks us to select the destination model; we'll select v3. Finally, we must name the mapping model. I named it the very descriptive FromV2toV3.

Now Xcode will do a best guess at the migration from v2 to v3 and display its results, as shown next. There's a lot of information in this view; let's go through it piece by piece. As we step through this view, keep in mind that the view represents the migration from the perspective of the destination model. Everything is described as coming *from* the source into the destination.

The *entity mappings* are on the left side of the view, just to the right of the project list. Each item in this list represents a part of the migration that will occur. They're not one-to-one with the number of entities that we have; we can actually have more or fewer mappings than we have entities. Specifically, as you'll see when we update this mapping model, we can have more than

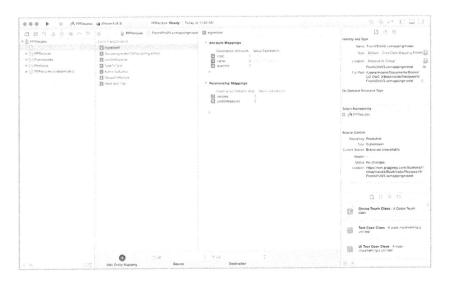

one mapping for an entity. In addition, if an entity is no longer represented in the new model, it may not have a mapping at all.

To the right of the entity mappings are the *attribute and relationship mappings*. The attribute mappings are located at the top of the view. This section of the view describes how the attributes of an entity are mapped from the source to the destination. Since we're looking at this from the perspective of the destination, this list includes every attribute that exists in the destination entity. Xcode has already prepopulated the attributes and taken a guess at where the attributes come from. Reviewing what has already been populated by Xcode, we can see how the attribute mappings work. Several variables are available for these mappings:

- $manager, which references the NSMigrationManagerKey
- $source, which references the NSMigrationSourceObjectKey
- $destination, which references the NSMigrationDestinationObjectKey
- $entityMapping, which references the NSMigrationEntityMappingKey
- $propertyMapping, which references the NSMigrationPropertyMappingKey
- $entityPolicy, which references the NSMigrationEntityPolicyKey

The relationship mappings are below the entity mappings. Like the attribute mappings, these resolve the relationships for the destination entity. Normally, these mappings resolve to an instance of an entity in the destination store that existed in the source store. To accomplish this, the mapping for the object at the other end of the relationship must be higher in the list (the list is migrated in order, top to bottom). Then it's a matter of configuring the mapping properly, as shown in the figure on page 57.

Customizing the Heavy/Manual Migration

So far, the migration we built doesn't do very much: it migrates the entities from the old store to the new store. We need to adjust the migration to make it perform the more complicated aspects of the migration, the ones that are beyond the abilities of the light migration.

The first part of this customization is to change the Type attribute on recipes that are currently set as Fish or Meat. To do this, we'll utilize the filter feature of the migration. First, select the RecipeToRecipe mapping. Next, open the Mapping Model inspector, which is utility view 3 in Xcode (⌘⌥3). In that inspector, we see a Filter Predicate field. This filter determines which entities are migrated. Utilizing a filter, we can migrate only those recipe entities that have their type set to something other than Fish or Meat. The setting is shown here:

However, this leaves our meat and fish recipes unmigrated. To include them, we first duplicate the RecipeToRecipe mapping (unfortunately by hand with the current version of Xcode) and change the filter to be *inclusive* of Meat and Fish. Then, in this second mapping, we change the Value Expression setting for the Type attribute to Entrée. Taking this step will migrate all of the meat and fish recipes and change the type to Entrée.

The second part of this migration is far more complex. For each RecipeIngredient, we want to either create a new Ingredient entity or link the destination RecipeIngredient to an existing Ingredient. In addition, for each Ingredient that we create, we want to create a UnitOfMeasure entity to go with it.

To complete this very complex migration, we'll have to resort to code. The mapping model editor isn't capable of handling the complexity we require for this next bit of the migration. Fortunately, we can step in and write the code to handle the migration directly. To set this up, we start off by modifying the mapping model. The first step is to delete the mappings for Ingredient and UnitOfMeasure. There's no corresponding entity in the source model, so no mapping is needed.

Next, we'll modify the RecipeIngredientToRecipeIngredient mapping. After selecting the RecipeIngredientToRecipeIngredient mapping, we need to look at the Mapping Model inspector and set a custom policy. The Custom Policy field tells the migration that instead of using its built-in migration policy (which will read from the mapping model), we're going to introduce custom code. This field accepts a class name that we'll set to RecipeIngredientToIngredientAndUnitOfMeasure.

NSEntityMigrationPolicy

Core Data will instantiate an instance of NSEntityMigrationPolicy for each mapping in the mapping model. NSEntityMigrationPolicy is designed to be subclassed so that we can override all or part of the migration. Several methods can be overridden in the subclass; in this example, we're overriding two methods: createDestinationInstancesForSourceInstance() and createRelationshipsForDestinationInstance()

Let's take a closer look at each of these.

createDestinationInstancesForSourceInstance()

The first method, createDestinationInstancesForSourceInstance(), is called for each entity in the source store that's associated with this migration policy. For example, during the migration of the RecipeIngredient entities and the creation of the Ingredient and UnitOfMeasure entities, this method would be called for each RecipeIngredient, and it'd be expected that at least an Ingredient entity would be created or associated with the incoming RecipeIngredient as a result.

The code to implement this breaks down as follows:

PPRecipesV3/PPRecipes/RecipeIngredientToIngredient.swift

```
override func createDestinationInstancesForSourceInstance(s: NSManagedObject,
  entityMapping mapping: NSEntityMapping,
  manager: NSMigrationManager) throws {
  let destMOC = manager.destinationContext
  guard let dEntityName = mapping.destinationEntityName else {
    fatalError("Destination entity name is nil")
  }

  guard let name = s.valueForKey("name") as? String else {
    fatalError("Source object did not have a value for 'name'")
  }
```

In the first part of the method, we're simply setting up references that will be needed later. Specifically, we're getting a reference to the destination NSManagedObjectContext, which we'll need to create new entities, the name of the destination entity, and, most importantly, the name value from the entity.

Since the incoming entity is a RecipeIngredient, the name value will be the name of the ingredient that we now want to reference.

PPRecipesV3/PPRecipes/RecipeIngredientToIngredient.swift

```
var userInfo: [NSObject:AnyObject]
if let managerUserInfo = manager.userInfo {
  userInfo = managerUserInfo
} else {
  userInfo = [NSObject:AnyObject]()
}

var ingredientLookup: [String:NSManagedObject]!
if let lookup = userInfo["ingredients"] as? [String:NSManagedObject] {
  ingredientLookup = lookup
} else {
  ingredientLookup = [String:NSManagedObject]()
  userInfo["ingredients"] = ingredientLookup
}

var uofmLookup: [String:NSManagedObject]!
if let lookup = userInfo["unitOfMeasure"] as? [String:NSManagedObject] {
  uofmLookup = lookup
} else {
  uofmLookup = [String:NSManagedObject]()
  userInfo["unitOfMeasure"] = uofmLookup
}
```

In this next section of code, we deal with the possibility that the Ingredient entity that we need to reference has already been created. Rather than doing a fetch against the destination context every time, we have a hash built up and stored within the NSMigrationManger. The NSMigrationManager has an NSDictionary called userInfo that's perfectly suited for this purpose. We first lazily initialize this dictionary, and then we lazily initialize another NSDictionary inside it to store references to the Ingredient entities using the name of the ingredient as the key. With this, we can make sure that each Ingredient is created only once.

For each Ingredient, we need to create or reference a UnitOfMeasure. We also grab a reference to the UnitOfMeasure lookup or create it if it hasn't been created yet.

PPRecipesV3/PPRecipes/RecipeIngredientToIngredient.swift

```
var dest = ingredientLookup[name]
if dest == nil {
  dest = NSEntityDescription.insertNewObjectForEntityForName(dEntityName,
    inManagedObjectContext: destMOC)
  dest!.setValue(name, forKey:"name")
  ingredientLookup[name] = dest

  guard let uofmName = s.valueForKey("unitOfMeasure") as? String else {
    fatalError("Unit of Measure name is nil")
  }
  var uofm = uofmLookup[uofmName]
  if uofm == nil {
    let eName = "UnitOfMeasure"
    uofm = NSEntityDescription.insertNewObjectForEntityForName(eName,
      inManagedObjectContext: destMOC)
    uofm!.setValue(uofmName, forKey:"name")
    dest!.setValue(uofm, forKey:"unitOfMeasure")
    uofmLookup[name] = uofm
  }
}
```

Next we attempt to locate the Ingredient in the lookup dictionary. If it isn't in the dictionary, we must create it and place it in the dictionary. If we need to create the Ingredient, we must resolve the UnitOfMeasure as well. Again, if it doesn't exist, we create it and put a reference to it in the lookup dictionary.

PPRecipesV3/PPRecipes/RecipeIngredientToIngredient.swift

```
  manager.userInfo = userInfo
}
```

The last thing that we have to do is to tell the manager about the association. Because the manager keeps track of all associations between the two NSManagedObjectContext objects, we need to inform it of this new entity that was just created and that it's associated with the source entity that was passed in. Once that's complete, we return YES, and we're done.

createRelationshipsForDestinationInstance()

In a properly designed data model, this method will rarely, if ever, be needed. The intention of this method (which is called in the second pass) is to build any relationships for the new destination entity that was created in the previous method. However, if all the relationships in the model are double-sided, this method isn't necessary because we already set up one side of them. If for some reason there's an entity in the model that is not double-sided, additional code would be required in this method to handle the one-sided relationship. Since we don't need that functionality in our model, we just leave the function empty.

PPRecipesV3/PPRecipes/RecipeIngredientToIngredient.swift

```
override func createRelationshipsForDestinationInstance(d: NSManagedObject,
  entityMapping mapping: NSEntityMapping,
  manager: NSMigrationManager) throws {
}
```

If you're thinking this is a lot of work for migration, well, you're right. Manual migrations require a great deal of effort on the part of the developer, and there isn't a lot of benefit to doing one. This, plus their poor performance, is the reason for my recommendation to avoid them at nearly any cost. However, no matter how hard we try to avoid it, sometimes heavy migration is the only answer. Fortunately, as we just examined, the option is available.

Fundamentals of Core Data Versioning

We've seen the nuts and bolts, but what's the magic behind all of this? How does the data migration actually work? As we already explored in Chapter 2, *Under the Hood*, on page 13, Core Data works with MOM (NSManagedObjectModel) objects that describe the data entities, their attributes, and their relationships.

Core Data versioning works with those same MOM objects but takes the design one step further.

Each entity version in each data model has a unique hash.

When Core Data loads a persistent store from disk, it resolves the matching hashes in the persistent store against the MOM objects included with the application.

If the matching MOM isn't flagged as the "current" MOM, data migration will then kick in.

How Data Migration Works

Core Data handles data migration in a very straightforward manner. When a persistent store needs to be migrated, Core Data performs three steps.

Copying the Entities with Attributes

In the first pass of the migration, Core Data creates new entities in the new persistent store for every entity in the old store. These entities have their attributes copied over, but not their relationships. During this phase, Core Data also keeps a reference to the old unique ID for each entity to be used in phase 2.

Creating Relationships Between the Entities

In the second pass, Core Data builds all the relationships between the entities based on the previous relationships. This is where the reference in phase 1 is used.

Validating the New Store

During the migration, all validation rules are turned off, and Core Data ignores the child classes defined in the MOM. Therefore, it's possible that some data validation rules may have been broken during the migration. In the final phase of the migration, Core Data goes back through the store and checks all the validation rules in order to ensure the data is in a valid state.

Model Versions and Hashes

The word *versioning* has been used throughout this chapter as well as other material to describe data migration in Core Data. Unfortunately, it's an inaccurate term. Versioning implies that there's an order or precedence to the models. This isn't accurate when it comes to data model versioning/migration in Core Data.

Entity Hashes

Instead of keeping track of a version number, creation date, or some other potentially chronological identifier, Core Data generates a hash for each entity in a model. The hashes are then stored within the persistent stores created with that model for later comparison. When a persistent store is loaded, the first thing Core Data does is retrieve the metadata from that store. Inside the metadata is a list of every entity type in the store, along with the hash for that entity. Core Data then compares that list of hashes against the hashes of the "current" MOM. If they match, everything is fine, and the store is loaded. If they don't match, Core Data checks the options on the load persistent store call to see whether automatic data migration is requested. If it isn't, an error message (shown in *Some Maintenance Before We Migrate*, on page 48) is presented to the user.

Changing the Hash Values

Surprisingly, not everything that changes inside a MOM causes the hash of the entities inside to change. There are actually quite a few things that we can do to a model that don't trigger data migration at all.

Changes That Alter the Entity Hash

If any of the following are changed on an entity, the entity will report a different hash.

- Name: Changing the name of the entity
- Inheritance: Changing the parent entity
- Persistent properties: Adding or removing a property

In addition, changing the following four properties will trigger a change to the entity hash.

- Name: The name of the property
- Optionality/read-only: Whether the property is optional or read-only
- Attribute type: The type of value stored
- Relationship: The destination, the minimum/maximum count, the delete rule, or the inverse

Changes That *Do Not* Alter the Entity Hash

The following changes to an entity will *not* trigger a change to the entity hash:

- Class name: Changing the NSManagedObject subclass
- Transient properties: Changing properties that aren't saved in the persistent store
- User info: Adding, removing, or changing the user info keys/values
- Validation predicates: Adding, removing, or changing the validation rules
- Default values: Adding, removing, or changing the default value of an attribute

In addition, the following changes to the properties of an entity will *not* change the hash of the entity:

- User info: Adding, removing, or changing the user info key/values
- Validation predicates: Adding, removing, or changing the validation rules

The general distinction between things that do and don't affect version hashes is whether the changes impact the store schema. Details such as the class name impact only the runtime, not the structure of the persistent data.

Mapping Models

If Core Data detects that an upgrade to the persistent store is needed, it looks for these three files in the application bundle:

- The MOM that matches the hash from the persistent store
- The current MOM
- The mapping model for those two MOM objects

Assuming that all three files are located, Core Data will then migrate the data in the persistent store from the old model to the current model. If Core Data can't locate a mapping model, it checks to see whether inferred (automatic) migration is turned on and attempts to do a lightweight migration. If inferred isn't turned on or if the migration is too complex for a lightweight migration, an error will occur. Otherwise, once the migration is complete, the stack (MOC, PS, and MOM) is fully initialized, and the application continues. This, of course, is the happy path, and there are several safeguards in place to allow the application developer to control failures.

It is of vital importance that the application developer test the migration as completely as possible and that every error condition be checked during development and testing. With the delay in application releases to the App Store, it has never been more important to ensure that the migration performs correctly every time.

Wrapping Up

We explored how to deal with changes and additions to our application and discussed data migration. In the next chapter, we'll take a look at how our applications perform and ways to tune them.

CHAPTER 5

Performance Tuning

Brent Simmons, creator of NetNewsWire, once shared a story about a user who filed a bug report about the poor startup performance of NetNewsWire. Upon discussion with that user, he discovered that the user had more than 900,000 unread RSS feeds! The lesson I took away from that story is to expect my users to put thousands of times as much data into my applications as I'd ever consider reasonable.

While we're working with Core Data, we need to consider the performance impacts of our design. We might test with a couple of dozen recipes and expect our users to load a couple hundred recipes into our application and test with those expectations. However, our users can't read our intentions or expectations. As soon as we ship the application, some user somewhere will load 100,000 recipes into it and then file a bug report that it performs poorly.

Persistent Store Types

Four types of repositories are included with the Core Data API: SQLite, XML, binary, and in-memory. (XML is available only on OS X, not on iOS.) In-memory is technically not a persistent store because it's never written out to disk. Binary is effectively a serialized version of the object graph written out to disk. The XML store writes out the object graph to a human-readable text file, and SQLite stores the object graph in a relational database. When working with an iOS project, you'll typically just use SQLite unless you have a specific reason to use one of the other store formats.

Atomic Stores

Atomic stores include XML, binary, and custom data stores. All of these stores are written to disk atomically; in other words, the entire data file is rewritten on every save. Although these store types have their advantages, they don't scale as well as the SQLite store. In addition, they're loaded fully into memory when they're accessed. This causes atomic stores to have a larger memory footprint than a SQLite store.

However, because they reside completely in memory while the application is running, atomic stores can be very fast, since the disk is hit only when the file is read into memory and when it's saved back out. SQLite, although still considered a fast store, is slower when dealing with smaller data sets because of its inherent disk access. The differences are measured in fractions of a second, so we can't expect a dramatic speed increase by using an atomic store. But if fractions of a second matter, it may be something to consider.

SQLite Persistent Store

In the most common cases, SQLite is the store option to use for application development. This is true on both iOS and OS X. SQLite is a software library that implements a self-contained, server-less, zero-configuration, transactional SQL database engine. SQLite is the most widely deployed SQL database engine in the world. The source code for SQLite is in the public domain.

Better Scaling

By utilizing a relational database as the persistent store, we no longer need to load the entire data set into memory to work with it. Because the data is being stored in a relational database, our application can scale to a very large size. SQLite itself has been tested with data sets measured in terabytes and can handle just about anything that we can realistically develop. Since we're loading only the data we want at a particular moment, SQLite keeps the memory footprint of our application quite low. Likewise, SQLite makes efficient use of its disk space and therefore has a small footprint on disk as well.

More Performance-Tuning Options

By working with a database instead of a flat file, we have access to many more performance-tuning options. For example, we can index the columns within our entities to enable faster predicates. We can also control exactly what gets loaded into memory. It's possible to get just a count of the objects, just the unique identifiers for objects, and so on. This flexibility allows us to tune the performance of our application more than any other store type. Because the SQLite store is the only format that's not fully loaded into memory, we get to control the data flow. All of the other formats require that the entire data file be loaded into memory before they can be used. The details of how to utilize these features are discussed in *Fetching*, on page 71.

Optimizing Your Data Model

When we design our data model, we need to consider several factors. Where we put our binary data can be extremely important because its size and storage location plays a key role in the performance of our application. Likewise, relationships must be carefully balanced and used appropriately. Also, entity inheritance, a powerful feature of Core Data, must be used with a delicate hand because the underlying structure may be surprising.

Although it's easy to think of Core Data as a database API, we must remember that it's not and that structuring the data with data normalization may not yield the most efficient results. In many cases, denormalizing the data can yield greater performance gains.

Where to Put Binary Data

One of the easiest ways to kill performance in a Core Data application is to stick large amounts of binary data into frequently accessed tables. For example, if we were to put the pictures of our recipes into the recipe table, we'd start seeing performance degradation after only a couple hundred recipes had been added. Every time we accessed a Recipe entity, we'd have to load its image data, even if we weren't going to display the image. Since our application displays all the recipes in a list, this means every image would reside in memory immediately upon launch and remain there until the application quit. Imagine this situation with a few thousand recipes!

But where do we draw the line? What's considered a small enough piece of binary data to fit into a table, and what shouldn't be put into the repository at all?

If you're developing an application that's targeting iOS 6.0 or greater (or Mac OS X 10.8 or greater), the answer is simple: turn on external binary storage in the model and let Core Data solve the problem for you. Just set the external record flag in the Data Model inspector panel, as shown here.

This feature instructs Core Data to determine how to store binary data. With this flag on, Core Data decides whether the image is small enough to store inside the SQLite file or whether it's too big and therefore should be stored on disk separately. In either case, the decision is an implementation detail from the perspective of our application. We access the binary data just like any other attribute on the entity.

If the application is still targeting an older version of the operating system (iOS or Mac OS X), then the application is responsible for dealing with binary data in a performant way.

Small Binary Data

Anything smaller than 100 kilobytes is considered to be small binary data. Icons or small avatars are a couple examples of data of this size. When working with something this small, you'll find it efficient to store it directly as a property value in its corresponding table. The performance impact of binary data this size is negligible. The transformable attribute type is ideal for this use.

Medium Binary Data

Medium binary data is anything larger than 100 kilobytes and smaller than 1 megabyte in size. Average-sized images and small audio clips are a few examples of data in this size range. Data of this size can also be stored directly in the repository. However, the data should be stored in its own table on the other end of a relationship with the primary tables. This allows the binary data to remain a fault until it's actually needed. In the previous recipe example, even though the Recipe entity would be loaded into memory for display, the image would be loaded only when it's needed by the UI.

SQLite has shown itself to be quite efficient at disk access. There are cases where loading data from the SQLite store can actually be faster than direct disk access. This is one of the reasons why medium binary data can be stored directly in the repository.

Large Binary Data

Large binary data is anything greater than 1 megabyte in size. Large images, audio files, and video files are just some examples of data of this size. Any binary data of this size should be stored on disk as opposed to in the repository. When you're working with data of this size, it's best to store its path information directly in the primary entity (such as the Recipe entity) and store the binary data in a known location on disk (such as in the Application Support subdirectory for your application).

Entity Inheritance

Entity inheritance is a very powerful feature within Core Data. It allows you to build an object-like inheritance tree in your data model. However, this feature comes at a rather large cost. For example, let's look at an example model that makes moderate use of entity inheritance:

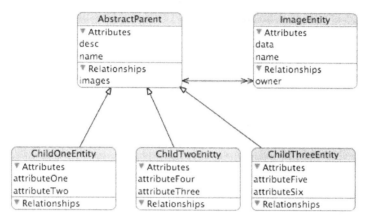

The object model itself looks quite reasonable. We're sharing name, desc, and a one-to-many relationship to the ImageEntity. However, the underlying table structure actually looks like this:

The reason for this is how Core Data handles the object model–to–relational table mapping. Instead of creating one table for each child object, Core Data creates one large table that includes all the properties for the parent entity as well as its children. The end result is an extremely wide and tall table in the database with a high percentage of empty values.

Although the entity inheritance feature of Core Data is extremely useful, we should be aware of what's going on underneath the object model to avoid a performance penalty. We shouldn't treat entity inheritance as an equal to object inheritance. There's certainly some overlap, but they aren't equal, and treating them as such will have a negative impact on the performance of the repository.

Denormalizing Data to Improve Performance

Although the most powerful persistent store available for Core Data is a database, we must always be conscious of the fact that Core Data isn't just a database. Core Data is an object hierarchy that can be persisted to a database format. The difference is subtle but important. Core Data is first a collection of objects that we use to display data in a user interface of some form and allow the user to access that data. Therefore, although database normalization might be the first place to look for performance improvements, we shouldn't take it too far. There are six levels of database normalization,[1] but a Core Data repository should rarely, if ever, be taken beyond the second level. In several cases we can gain a greater performance benefit by denormalizing the data.

Search-Only Properties

Searching within properties can be quite expensive. For properties that have a large amount of text or, worse, Unicode text, a single search field can cause a huge performance hit. One way to improve this situation is to create a derived attribute based on the text in an entity. For example, searching in our description property of the Recipe entity can potentially be very expensive if the user has verbose descriptions and/or uses Unicode characters in the description.

To improve the performance of searches in this field, we could create a second property on the Recipe entity that strips the Unicode characters from the description and also removes common words such as *a, the, and*, and so on. If we then perform the search on this derived property, we can drastically improve search performance.

The downside to using search-only properties is that we need to maintain them. Every time the description field is edited, we have to update the derived property as well.

Expensive Calculations

In a normalized database, calculated values aren't stored. It's considered cheaper to recalculate the value as needed than to store it in the database. However, from a user experience point of view, the opposite can frequently be true. In cases where the calculation takes a human-noticeable amount of time, it may very well be better for the user if we were to store that calculation in the entity and recalculate it only when one of its dependent values has changed. For example, if we store the first and last names of a user in our Core Data repository, it might make sense to store the full name as well.

---

1. See http://en.wikipedia.org/wiki/Database_normalization for details.

Intelligent Relationships

Relationships in a Core Data model are like salt in a cooking recipe. Too much and you ruin the recipe; too little and something is missing. Fortunately, there are some simple rules we can follow when it comes to relationships in a Core Data repository.

Follow the Object Model

Core Data is first and foremost an object model. The entities in our model should represent the data as accurately as possible. Just because a value might be duplicated across several objects (or rows from the database point of view) doesn't mean it should be extruded into its own table. Many times it's more efficient for us to store that string several times over in the entity itself than to traverse a relationship to get it.

Traversing a relationship is generally more expensive than accessing an attribute on the entity. Therefore, if the value being stored is simple, it's better to leave it in the entity it's associated with.

Separate Commonly Used from Rarely Used Data

If the object design calls for a one-to-many relationship or a many-to-many relationship, we should definitely create a relationship for it. This is usually the case where the data is more than a single property or contains binary data or would be difficult to properly model inside the parent object. For example, if we have a user entity, it's more efficient to store the user's address in its own object as opposed to having several attributes in the user object for address, city, state, postal code, and so on.

A balance needs to be carefully maintained between what's stored on the other end of a relationship and what's stored in the primary entity. Crossing key paths is more expensive than accessing attributes, but creating objects that are very wide also slows down data access.

Fetching

Fetching is the term used to describe the resolving of NSManagedObject objects from the repository. When we retrieve an NSManagedObject, it's "fetched" into memory, and we can then access its properties. To help us utilize memory efficiently, fetching may not always happen all at once. Specifically, when we're using a SQLite store, it's quite possible that an object we think is in memory is only on disk and has yet to be read into memory. Likewise, objects that we think we're done with may actually still sit in a cache.

To demonstrate the differences in the ways that we can load data into memory from our SQLite Store, let's look at an older Apple demonstration application from a previous WWDC called GoFetch. (The source code for this application is available as part of this book's download.) The entire goal of this application is to generate a large amount of random data and let us control how it's fetched back into memory. Each fetch is then timed to demonstrate the speed of various options. These tests were performed with 3,417 records in the SQLite repository.

Loading NSManagedObjectID Objects Only

The smallest amount of data that we can retrieve as part of an NSFetchRequest is just the NSManagedObjectID. The NSManagedObjectID is the unique identifier for the record and contains no content. In the test discussed earlier, it took the test machine 0.004 seconds to retrieve 3,417 records from disk.

There's only one change required to retrieve just NSManagedObjectID objects instead of full NSManagedObject objects.

```
let request = NSFetchRequest(entityName: "Person")
request.resultType = .ManagedObjectIDResultType
```

By changing the resultType to ManagedObjectIDResultType, our call to executeFetchRequest: returns an array of NSManagedObjectID objects instead of NSManagedObject objects.

Loaded as a Fault

The next smallest amount of data we can retrieve is referred to as a *faulted* NSManagedObject. What this means is the NSFetchRequest returns an NSArray of NSManagedObject objects, but those objects contain only the NSManagedObjectID. All the properties and relationships are empty or in a faulted state. As soon as an attribute is accessed, *all of the attributes on that object are loaded in.* Likewise, as soon as a relationship is accessed, all the NSManagedObject objects on the other end of that relationship are loaded in as faults. Performing the same query as earlier in this configuration returned the 3,417 records in 0.007 seconds. Faults will be discussed in further in *Faulting*, on page 74.

To disable the fetching of attributes as part of the NSFetchRequest, we need to configure the fetch prior to executing it.

```
let request = NSFetchRequest(entityName: "Person")
request.includesPropertyValues = false
```

Although this seems like a great solution, it can be a bit of a trap. Because this configuration returns empty skeletons, each object gets loaded from disk individually. This is *significantly* slower than loading all the objects needed at once. However, the time to load the objects is spread out and can be less noticeable to the user. For raw speed, I recommend that you load all the data for the objects in one pass.

Loading Property Values

The next step up from faulted NSManagedObject objects is to prefetch their property values. This won't retrieve the objects on the other sides of relationships. Performing this query took 0.021 seconds for the 3,417 records in the test repository.

Retrieving NSManagedObject objects with attributes populated is the default for NSFetchRequest.

```
let request = NSFetchRequest(entityName: "Person")
```

This option is a good middle ground between fetching faults and some of the following choices. In situations where only the object requested needs to be displayed right away and its relationships aren't needed right away, this can be the most efficient solution.

Loading Relationships

The next step up in the scale of loading data is to prefetch the relationships while loading the targeted entities. This doesn't fetch them as fully formed but as faults. This step up can have a significant impact on the performance of a Core Data application. In the test, this fetch took 1.166 seconds to retrieve 3,417 objects, each with only a *single* object on the other side of a one-to-one relationship. With a more complex data model, this becomes an even larger performance hit.

Fortunately, this option gives us some fine-grained control over which relationships to load. This would allow us to, for example, load only the addresses associated with a person and skip over their images, phone numbers, and so on. Accomplishing this requires passing an array of String objects with the names of the relationships to load.

```
let request = NSFetchRequest(entityName: "Person")
request.relationshipKeyPathsForPrefetching = ["addresses"]
```

In this example code, we create a new array that has one String within it that corresponds to the name of the relationship within the Person entity. We can get even more clever with this request by using a keypath in the array and specifying a second level of objects to include in the fetch. For example, if our

Address entities had a relationship to a postal code lookup table that contained the city and state, we could change the `NSArray` creation line to the following:

```
request.relationshipKeyPathsForPrefetching = ["addresses",
"addresses.postalCode"]
```

That would cause Core Data to retrieve two levels of relationships as faults. In addition, this call does check for duplication before executing the requests and thereby can be used safely when mixing keypaths. In other words, the `postalCode` relationship, which is probably many to many, won't be retrieved more than once.

NSFetchRequest and Disk Access

Every time an `NSFetchRequest` is executed, it hits the disk. This is an important point to keep in mind when we're working with `NSManagedObject` objects. If we're doing joins, adding objects to a relationship, and so on, it might seem easier and cleaner to perform an `NSFetchRequest` to check whether the object is already in the relationship or check for a similar function, but that action can hurt performance significantly. Even if we have all the relevant objects in memory, an `NSFetchRequest` is still going to hit the disk. It's far more efficient for us to use an `NSPredicate` against a collection that's already in memory.

You've seen in this section that with a SQLite persistent store, you have a lot of control over how your data is loaded into memory. You can tailor the load to fit your exacting needs. All of these options can be a bit overwhelming, but there's one good rule of thumb. Try to load *only* the data you need at that moment in one pass. Every fetch request can take quite a bit of time, and since the fetch requests are normally performed on the main thread, they can damage the user experience of your application.

Faulting

Firing faults individually is one of the most common, if not the most common, cause for the poor performance of Core Data applications. Faults are a double-edged sword that can make great improvements to the speed and performance of our applications or can drag the performance down to the depths of the unusable. The single most valuable performance improvement we can make to a Core Data application is to make sure we're fetching only the data we need when we need it. If we fetch too little, our application will feel unresponsive. If we fetch too much, our application will stall and potentially be killed by the operating system.

Orders of Magnitude

Disk access is significantly slower than accessing memory. The times measured for each is *six orders of magnitude* different. This translates into disk access being roughly 1 million times slower than accessing data that's stored in memory, as illustrated:

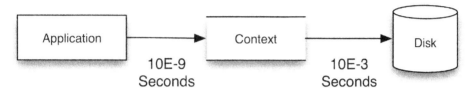

Although the actual retrieval times are closer to a few thousand times slower, the point is still clear. Avoid accessing the disk if possible. However, when we have no choice but to access the disk, we must attempt to get everything we need in one pass. Repeated small requests to the disk are significantly slower than one larger request.

Prefetching

In *Fetching*, on page 71, we reviewed the different ways we can retrieve the data from disk. To expand on that, consider each request we make from the NSManagedObjectContext and try to retrieve all the data in one request that the user is going to want to view. For example, if the user will be editing a user record, load that user and all its relationships at once. This will be significantly faster than grabbing the Person entity and then going back to grab three Address entities, then two Phone entities, and so on. Use the relationship prefetching option of NSFetchRequest to grab all of them at once.

If we can predict what the user is going to want to see and load it ahead of the user's request, the overall user experience will be vastly improved. As we're developing our applications, we need to look at each window, view, or sheet and ask, "What information will this part present?" and make sure all of that information is either already in memory or loaded at once. Having said that, we need to balance this with information overload, as discussed in *Access Patterns*, on page 77.

Warming Up the Cache

It's possible to preload the data into the cache so that it's in memory when we need it. The easiest way to perform this step is to execute a full fetch on a background thread. For example, on launch of our recipe application, we could launch a background thread to retrieve all the Recipe entities. This would allow us to fill the cache with the Recipe entities that we know are going to be presented to the user, in turn allowing the main thread to grab those recipes from the cache instead of the disk and give the user a smoother-running application in the process. The magic behind this is based on how the NSPersistentStoreCoordinator works. Whenever any request on any thread is performed, the data is held in the NSPersistentStoreCoordinator as part of its cache. When another request is made, no matter what thread it came from, for that same data it's retrieved from the cache instead of requiring another hit to the disk.

Saving

The numbers discussed in *Orders of Magnitude*, on page 75 also apply to writing the data back out to the disk. In fact, writing to the disk is even slower than reading from it. Therefore, it's more efficient for us to save data back out to disk in batches. Saving after every record change causes our entire application to feel sluggish to the user. Likewise, doing a huge write while the application is attempting to exit gives the appearance that our application has stopped responding and risks data loss. As with most things when it comes to performance tuning, be aware of your saves and how much data you're saving and how frequently. Try to do saves during logical pauses in the application flow.

Deleting

It may come as a surprise, but deleting an object can cause a performance issue. Let's review the data model from Chapter 4, *Versioning and Migration*, on page 47. Imagine that in this later version of our application we want to delete a recipe from the repository. When we delete the recipe, we have a cascade rule set up to delete all the associated RecipeIngredient entities as well. We also need to touch the Author entity, Ingredient entity, and UnitOfMeasure entity, as shown in the figure on page 77.

It's obvious why we need to touch the RecipeIngredient entity, but why do we need to access all the others? This is because of the relationships between the entities. For each relationship, we need to validate the relationship after the delete and confirm that there are no dangling references. If these objects aren't currently in memory, then the NSManagedObjectContext must retrieve them from the disk to accomplish all of this.

Therefore, when we're doing deletes, especially large deletes, it can be a performance improvement to fetch all the relationships prior to the delete.

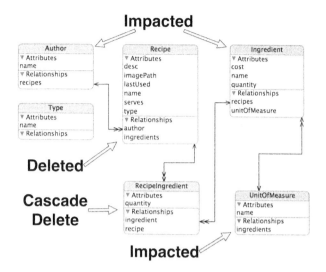

Faulting and Disk Access

Firing a fault doesn't always mean that the data is going to be read from disk. Depending on how we've requested the data in the first place or what happened earlier in the NSManagedObject object's life span, it's quite possible that the data will be loaded from cache instead.

Likewise, faulting an NSManagedObject doesn't guarantee that it will be written back out to disk, nor does it guarantee that it will be removed from the cache. If the object has no changes, then there's nothing to write to disk, and it's quite possible it will remain in the cache for an unknown period of time.

Easily one of the best ways to check to see whether the firing of a fault is in fact causing disk access is to monitor our application with instruments. By using the Core Data template, we can use the "cache miss" instrument to check for disk hits. If we're getting far more calls to the disk than expected, we need to consider refactoring the code.

Access Patterns

Improving performance within Core Data isn't necessarily only about the repository and order of loading the data. We can do a number of things within the user interface to help performance as well.

Searching the repository can be absolute murder on performance. Whether we're searching at the request of the user or performing a search in the background, we need to be very careful to avoid impacting the performance of our application.

Order Is Important

Just like any conditional, the order of the logic is important. Simple equality is faster than inclusions such as *in*, *contains*, and so on. When building the predicate, try to order the logic from left to right, simple to complex. This process allows Core Data to fail quickly and improve the search performance.

Unicode and Regular Expressions

Unicode is very expensive to work with when we're searching. As suggested earlier in *Search-Only Properties*, on page 70, try to avoid searching against Unicode directly. It's cheaper to keep a derived value that strips off the Unicode than it is to do frequent searches against the Unicode text.

Likewise, regular expressions are expensive. If a situation calls for one, try to put it at the far-right end of the NSPredicate, as discussed previously.

Limit Queries Across Relationships

Searching across objects that are joined by a relationship can be very expensive. Although it's impressive to search against person.address.postalCode.city, it may not be the most efficient way to solve the problem. Consider reversing the query or breaking it down into several smaller queries to reduce the complexity of the underlying SQL. When we're working with a SQLite back end, all of our NSPredicate calls turn into SQL before hitting the database. The less complex that SQL is, the faster it will run. It may very well be faster to get an NSArray of all the Address objects within a specific city and then perform the rest of the query against that NSArray than it would be to traverse three relationships in one call.

Wrapping Up

A busy user interface is more than just a poor user experience; it also impacts the performance of the application. When we display a large amount of data on the screen, we must keep that information in memory, which in turn means we must load a large amount of data from disk all in one go. It's far better to break up an application user interface into consumable chunks of information than it is to try to display every last bit on the screen at once.

The careful use of tabs, sheets, and panels can improve the feel of a user interface, and that will in turn improve the performance. By splitting the user interface into smaller pieces, we have finer-grained control over what data gets loaded when, and we can reduce our disk access to manageable chunks. Keep it simple.

Threading

Multithreading is one of the great double-edged swords of programming. If it's done correctly, it can be a real boon to your application; done incorrectly, it leads to strange, unreproducible errors in the application. Multithreading has a tendency to polarize developers: they either swear that it's necessary for any application to perform properly or declare it's to be avoided at all costs. The truth, of course, is somewhere in the middle. Multithreading is a vital piece of the overall performance puzzle. While adding more threads won't automatically make your application faster, it can make your application "feel" faster to the user. That perception is what we'll focus on in this chapter.

It's a common misconception among developers that the point of adding threads to an application is to improve performance. Although there's no argument that proper threading support can improve performance in an application, treating threading like a silver bullet is a sure way to disaster.

Threading should be introduced to an application as part of the design process, whenever there's a situation where the application can or should be doing more than one thing. Any situation during the application design where an operation is needed but the user doesn't need to wait on that operation is a perfect situation for an additional thread.

Here are some common operations that fall into this category:

- Exporting data to a web service
- Importing data from a web service
- Recalculating data (totals and balances)
- Caching images
- Caching videos

And the list goes on. In addition to these concepts there's the concept of anticipating the user and what data the user is going to want next. If, for example, you're developing a news application, it makes sense to load the full news articles, images, videos, and so forth while the user is still scrolling through the list of articles. Ideally your application will have the data loaded and ready to display before the user selects it.

When an application can correctly predict what data a user is going to want to see before the user requests it, that application reaches a whole new level in user experience.

The purpose of adding threads to your application is to improve user experience by offloading work the user doesn't need to be blocked by, as well as to predictively load data before the user needs it.

With that goal for threading in mind, let's look at how to use Core Data in a multithreaded environment.

Threading and Core Data

Throughout the life of the Core Data framework, the approach to using Core Data with threading has changed many times. Originally there was no support for threading other than "figure it out," which evolved into the basic rule of "A context and its data must stay on one thread."

With the introduction of iOS 5.0 and OS X 10.8, Core Data began utilizing GCD (Grand Central Dispatch) and blocks that were introduced to the overall system in the previous generation. To further define how threading should be approached with Core Data, the threading model was again refined in iOS 8.0 and OS X 10.10 and yet again in iOS 9.0 and OS X 10.11.

With these changes, the threading model for Core Data has become a binary decision. We can use Core Data on the main thread (also known as the UI thread), or we can use Core Data on a background thread for things that don't directly impact the UI thread, which is a binary question. This evolution has been an incredibly good thing for Core Data. The question of how to use threads, and when, has been boiled down to a single Boolean question.

Starting with iOS 9.0 and OS X 10.11, the generic -init method of the NSManagedObjectContext has been deprecated. Previously, when you called this initializer you were returned an instance of NSManagedObjectContext that was *associated* with the thread that created it.

This type of creation was one of parts of Core Data and threading that confused developers and was finally removed. Now when you want a new instance of NSManagedObjectContext, you have to explicitly specify what thread that the NSManagedObjectContext will be associated with.

```
let moc = NSManagedObjectContext(concurrencyType: ${XXX})
```

With this initializer we have two options we can pass in for ${XXX}:

- .MainQueueConcurrencyType: This option will configure the NSManagedObjectContext so that it can only be run on the main queue/thread.
- .PrivateQueueConcurrencyType: This option will configure the NSManagedObjectContext so that it can only be run on a private queue/thread.

As mentioned, this is now a binary decision when we're initializing a NSManagedObjectContext. If the NSManagedObjectContext is going to be used with the user interface, then the NSMainQueueConcurrencyType will be used. Otherwise you *must* use the NSPrivateQueueConcurrencyType.

Working on the Main Queue

In general, working on the main queue has not changed from the original design. Assuming you're working with an NSManagedObjectContext that's configured to run on the main queue, you'd access that NSManagedObjectContext the exact same way as before.

The big difference is when your code is on *another* queue and you need to do some data work on the main queue. Getting that work onto the main queue has changed, fortunately for the better. This improvement is in the form of two methods: performBlock: and performBlockAndWait:.

Introducing performBlock:

The goal of performBlock: is to guarantee that a block of code is being executed on the correct queue, which is the queue that the NSManagedObjectContext is associated with. Therefore, if you have a block of code that you need to execute on the main queue against the NSManagedObjectContext associated with the main queue, you can do the following:

```
let moc = ... //Reference ot main queue context
moc.performBlock({
  let request = NSFetchRequest()
  // Define the request
  do {
    let results = try moc.executeRequest(request)
    // Do something with the results
  } catch {
    fatalError("Error fetching: \(error)")
  }
})
```

In this example you retrieve a reference to the existing NSManagedObjectContext that's instantiated against the main queue. From there you call performBlock:, and inside that block is where you do *all* of the work that needs to be performed on the main queue against Core Data.

The call to performBlock: takes the block of code and puts in the "todo" list for the queue associated with the NSManagedObjectContext that it's called against. As soon as that queue gets to the block of code, it will be executed. Generally, the execution happens right away. But if that queue is busy with another task (for example, another block of code to execute), then the block will be performed later.

Calling performBlock: isn't a "blocking" call. That means the queue that calls performBlock: won't be halted or paused and the line of code after the performBlock: call will be executed immediately—most likely before the block is executed.

What this also means is that the performBlock: call is re-entrant. While you're inside one call to performBlock: you can kick off another call. Your second call to performBlock: is guaranteed to be executed *after* the first call. Therefore, you could do something clever like this:

```
let moc = ... //Reference to main queue context
moc.performBlock({
  moc.performBlock({
    do {
      try moc.save()
    } catch {
      fatalError("Failed to save: \(error)")
    }
  })
  let request = NSFetchRequest()
  //... Define the request
  do {
    let results = try moc.executeRequest(request)

    // Do something with the results
  } catch {
    fatalError("Error fetching: \(error)")
  }
})
```

And the save() call would be executed *after* the data manipulation code. This effectively gives you a try/finally pattern.

Introducing performBlockAndWait:

There are plenty of situations where you want to execute code on the main queue but you want your background queue (aka non-main queue) to wait for that execution to be completed. That's where the API performBlockAndWait: is used. The parameters are exactly the same but the behavior is a bit different.

The primary difference is that this API call will *block* the calling queue until the block is completed. Which means that performBlockAndWait: is *not* re-entrant.

Working off the Main Queue

Now that threading with Core Data has been reduced to a binary question, the *other* type of NSManagedObjectContext we will take a look at is the NSPrivate-QueueConcurrencyType.

The singular difference between the two context types is what queue the context is associated with. When you're working with an NSMainQueueConcurren-cyType context, the context automatically associates itself with the main queue. When you initialize an NSPrivateQueueConcurrencyType context, the context will associate itself with a non-main queue that's *private* to the context.

Private means that you cannot access that queue directly. Calling dispatch_sync or dispatch_async on that queue is against the API. So, the *only* way to interact with a private queue context is through performBlock: and performBlockAndWait:.

This difference also means that *any* interaction with the private queue context must be inside a performBlock: or performBlockAndWait: call. The three exceptions to that rule are initialization, parentContext, and persistentStoreCoordinator. Any other interaction with a private queue context must be wrapped in a block.

As with a main queue context, any objects created or retrieved from a private queue context can only be accessed on that private queue. If you attempt to access those objects outside of the code block, you're violating the thread constraint rules of Core Data and will run into data integrity issues.

Interqueue Communication

Since objects created with or retrieved from a context can only be accessed on the queue associated with that context, the challenge becomes passing references to those objects between queues. This is arguably the biggest area where multiple threads with Core Data cause people the most issues.

If a reference to an object must be passed between queues, the best way to achieve that hand-off is via the object's objectID property. This property is designed to be safe to access from multiple queues and is a unique identifier to the object.

A Note About the NSManagedObjectID

This unique identifier is generally only guaranteed to reference the object for the current life cycle of the application. While the -objectID can be persisted through various means, that approach isn't recommended. There are several external actions that can void the reference and cause it to no longer function.

Once you have a reference to the objectID associated with an NSManagedObject, you can retrieve another reference to that NSManagedObject from another context through a few methods:

- objectWithID: will return an object for any objectID passed to it. The danger with this method is that it's *guaranteed* to return an object, even if it has to return an empty shell pointing to a nonexisting object. This can happen if an objectID is persisted and restored in a later application life cycle.

- existingObjectWithID: is a preferred method to use because it will give back an object if it exists and will return nil if no object exists for the objectID. The slight negative with this method is that it can perform I/O if the object isn't cached.

- objectRegisteredForID: is the third option for object retrieval with objectID. This method will return the object if it's already registered in the context that the method is being called against. Generally, this method is only useful if you already know that the object has previously been fetched in the context.

In addition to object hand-off between queues (the passing of an object reference from one queue to another), there's the handling of changes performed on a queue. By default, one context won't notify another context if an object has been changed. It's the responsibility of the developer to notify the other context of any changes. This is handled through the notification system.

Every time save() is called against an NSManagedObjectContext, that context will broadcast a few notifications. The one that's useful for cross-context notifications is NSManagedObjectContextDidSaveNotification. That notification is fired once the save has completed successfully and the notification object that's passed along includes all of the objects that were a part of the save.

If you have two contexts that you wish to keep in sync with each other, you can subscribe to this notification and then instruct the other context to consume the notification. For example, imagine in your data controller you have two contexts—contextA and contextB—that you wish to keep in sync. Once those contexts have been initialized, you can subscribe to their notifications:

```
let center = NSNotificationCenter.defaultCenter()
center.addObserver(self, selector: "contextASave:",
    name: NSManagedObjectContextDidSaveNotification, object: contextA)
center.addObserver(self, selector: "contextBSave:",
    name: NSManagedObjectContextDidSaveNotification, object: contextB)
```

In general you want notification observations to be as narrowly focused as possible. Although you could pass nil to the object: parameter, there would be no guarantee of who was broadcasting the notification, and you'd then need to filter inside the receiving method. By defining what objects we're willing to accept notifications from, we don't need to write defensive code in the receiving method and, as a result, we keep the receiving methods cleaner.

Once you see this notification, you can then consume it:

```
func contextASave(notif: NSNotification) {
    contextB?.performBlock({
        self.contextB?.mergeChangesFromContextDidSaveNotification(notif)
    })
}
func contextBSave(notif: NSNotification) {
    contextA?.performBlock({
        self.contextA?.mergeChangesFromContextDidSaveNotification(notif)
    })
}
```

With this implementation, every time contextA is saved, contextB will be notified and every time contextB is saved, contextA will be notified. Note that these mergeChangesFromContextDidSaveNotification: calls should be wrapped in a performBlock: to guarantee that they're being processed on the proper queue.

Note that while the mergeChangesFromContextDidSaveNotification: is being consumed, the context is also notifying any of its observers that those changes are taking place. This means that there can be side effects to this call.

For example, if the contextA has an NSFetchedResultsController associated with it and that NSFetchedResultsController has some expensive cell drawing associated with it, we can expect to see a performance hotspot while consuming notifications. The reason for that is that the processing of these notifications isn't threaded and the call to mergeChangesFromContextDidSaveNotification: won't return until all of the cells associated with that NSFetchedResultsController have completed *their* processing. Worse, since the NSFetchedResultsController and associated cells are on the main queue the *entire* application's user interface is effectively halted while these changes are being processed. This can result in some very surprising user interface delays. The best way to avoid these performance issues is to keep the cells from taking too long to draw or to break the save notification up into smaller units that can be processed faster.

Parent/Child NSManagedObjectContext Design

In the previous section, you saw how to consume changes from one context into another. With iOS 5.0, Core Data added another option to handle change notifications. Instead of having every context talk directly to the NSPersistentStore-Coordinator, we can chain contexts together in a parent/child design.

Each child context will request objects from its parent context, and if that parent context doesn't have the objects requested, it will pass that request up the chain until it hits the NSPersistentStoreCoordinator and I/O is performed. However, if the parent context does have a reference to the desired objects, then they're returned to the child without I/O being performed.

Further, when a child makes a change to an object and then calls save:, *no I/O is performed as a result of that call.* This means that child contexts can make changes to objects and pass them to their parent without a performance penalty. Also, change notifications are handled automatically by the context, so you don't need to observe the notifications and then consume them.

To define a context as a child of another context, the setup is slightly different:

```
let moc = ... //The existing context
let type = NSManagedObjectContextConcurrencyType.PrivateQueueConcurrencyType
let child = NSManagedObjectContext(concurrencyType: type)
child.parentContext = moc
```

Instead of the child being associated with the NSPersistentStoreCoordinator via the persistentStoreCoordinator property, it's associated with another context via a call to the parentContext property. This tells the NSManagedObjectContext that when it makes a request or saves an object that those requests and/or changes need to be pushed to the parent context.

The result of this is that it's possible to have contexts that can make changes and push them up to another context without having to write out to disk via the NSPersistentStoreCoordinator. If the child context is a child of the main queue context that's associated with the user interface, then the child context can process data on a background queue (via being created as an NSPrivateQueueCon-currencyType context), and then when a save occurs, the user interface is notified *immediately.*

There are a few things to be aware of with this design. First, the changes aren't actually persisted until they're passed to an NSPersistentStoreCoordinator. This means that if a change is made in a child context and passed to the main queue context but the main queue context isn't saved before the application exits, that change will be lost. If the application is set up to save the main queue context on exit, this isn't normally an issue unless the application terminates abruptly.

The second issue is that this concept of automatic change notification only goes one direction: from child to parent. If a change is made in the parent and even if the parent is saved, the child isn't notified of that change. If the child already had a reference to the object that was changed, the child wouldn't receive those updates and this could potentially cause a merge conflict if the child also attempted to alter that object.

There are many benefits to using this parent/child design. First, without having to listen for notifications, the amount of code that needs to be written is reduced. As part of that, the notification process is much faster. The contexts talking internally is going to be faster than code that you can write that talks to them externally.

Since child contexts request their data from their parent first, they can be much faster in retrieving objects if those objects are already in memory. For situations where you want to process data that already exists in memory, it makes sense to spawn a private child context and let that context process the data off the main queue. Ideally, there will be no I/O during that data processing.

Yet another benefit is in data consumption. When a request is made to the Internet and the resulting data needs to be consumed, it can be consumed with a child context with minimal impact to the main queue and user interface.

In the next few sections, we'll demonstrate using the parent/child design.

Export Operation

In the first demonstration, we'll add the ability to export recipes from Core Data so that they can be shared. We'll create an NSOperation, which will create its own NSManagedObjectContext and use it to copy the selected recipes into a JSON structure, which can then be used by the application in several ways (uploaded to a server, emailed to a friend, and so on).

To implement this addition to our application, we need to make a few changes to the user interface. We want to add a button to the UINavigationBar that's a generic action item. When the button is tapped, it will display an action sheet and give the user an option to mail the recipe (other options can be added later), as shown in the following figure on page 88.

To accomplish this, we first add the button in the storyboard and associate the button with a new method called -action:. Inside the -action: method, we construct a UIAlertController and present it to the user.

PPRecipes/PPRecipes/PPRDetailViewController.swift

```
func action(sender: AnyObject) {
  let controller = UIAlertController()
  var action = UIAlertAction(title: "Export Recipe", style: .Default) {
    (action) in
    self.mailRecipe()
  }
  controller.addAction(action)
  action = UIAlertAction(title: "Cancel", style: .Cancel, handler: nil)
  controller.addAction(action)
  presentViewController(controller, animated: true, completion: nil)
}
```

If the user clicked Cancel, we do nothing. Otherwise, the mailRecipe function will be called through the action handler.

Building the Operation

When the user taps Mail Recipe, the mailRecipe function gets called from the UIAlertController action.

```
func mailRecipe() {
  guard let mo = recipeMO else {
    fatalError("Unexpected nil recipe")
  }
  let operation = PPRExportOperation(mo, completionHandler: {
    (data, error) in
    if error != nil {
      fatalError("Export failed: \(error)")
    }
    //Mail the data to a friend
  })
  NSOperationQueue.mainQueue().addOperation(operation)
}
```

In the mailRecipe method, we construct a PPRExportOperation instance, passing it the recipe. We also give the PPRExportOperation a closure to report back when the operation has completed. The completion block is issued to handle the results of the export operation. Note that the closure receives back both an NSData and an NSError. If the operation was successful, the NSData is populated. If the operation failed for any reason, the NSData is nil, and the NSError is populated. In a production application, we'd want to respond to the error. For now, we have a developer-level logic check to capture the error.

The next step is to build the PPRExportOperation. The goal of the operation is to accept a single recipe and turn it into a JSON structure. When the export is complete, the operation will execute the closure and pass the resulting data back to the caller.

The initializer for our export operation needs to retain only the NSManagedObjectID of the incoming NSManagedObject. Because the init() method is being called on the queue on which the the incoming NSManagedObject was created (the main queue), we can access its methods. Once we're in our own -main method, we can no longer access it. However, the NSManagedObjectID is thread-safe and can cross the boundary. So, we grab it now and hold onto it in a property. We pass the entire NSManagedObject so that we can also grab a reference to the NSManagedObjectContext without having to explicitly request it.

In addition to the NSManagedObjectID, the PPRExportOperation stores a reference to the passed-in closure and unwraps the NSManagedObjectContext associated with the recipe.

PPRecipes/PPRecipes/ExportImportHandler.swift

```swift
init(_ aRecipe: PPRecipeMO, completionHandler aHandler: (data: NSData?,
  error: NSError?) -> Void) {

  guard let moc = aRecipe.managedObjectContext else {
    fatalError("Recipe has no context")
  }
  self.parentContext = moc
  recipeID = aRecipe.objectID
  handler = aHandler
  super.init()
}
init(data: NSData, context: NSManagedObjectContext,
  handler: (error: NSError?) -> Void) {
  incomingData = data
  parentContext = context
  super.init()
}
```

Once the operation is started, we must perform a couple of startup tasks. First, we need to create the child context.

PPRecipes/PPRecipes/ExportImportHandler.swift

```swift
override func main() {
  let t = NSManagedObjectContextConcurrencyType.PrivateQueueConcurrencyType
  let localMOC = NSManagedObjectContext(concurrencyType: t)
  localMOC.parentContext = parentContext
```

Now that we have a private NSManagedObjectContext, we need to kick off a perform-BlockAndWait: and then retrieve a local copy of the recipe. In this situation we want to have the operation block until the processing is completed so that the operation isn't destroyed by ending early.

A call to objectWithID: returns a local copy of the NSManagedObject. Since we know the object already exists in the parent NSManagedObjectContext, it's safe to assume that there will be no I/O in retrieving this object.

Conversion to JSON

Once we have a local copy of the recipe, we need to turn it into a JSON structure. To do that, we must first convert the NSManagedObject into a dictionary. However, we don't want to grab just the top-level object; we also want the author, the ingredients, and so on. To get all of those, we'll have to do a bit of recursive work.

PPRecipes/PPRecipes/ExportImportHandler.swift

```
func moToDictionary(mo: NSManagedObject) -> [String:AnyObject] {
  var dict = [String:AnyObject]()
  let entity = mo.entity

  for (key, value) in entity.attributesByName {
    dict[key] = value
  }
```

The first part of the conversion involves grabbing all of the attributes (strings, numbers, dates) from the NSManagedObject and placing them into a dictionary. By utilizing KVC, we can do this with a small amount of code. We first ask the NSEntityDescription for all of the attributes by name, and then we iterate over the resulting dictionary and add them to our dictionary.

PPRecipes/PPRecipes/ExportImportHandler.swift

```
let relationships = entity.relationshipsByName
for (name, relDesc) in relationships {
  if let skip = relDesc.userInfo?[PPExportRelationship] as? NSString {
    if skip.boolValue {
      continue
    }
  }
```

Next, we must deal with the relationships. Just as with the attributes, we can find out the name of each relationship from the NSEntityDescription. By looping over the resulting dictionary, we can process each relationship. However, to make sure we aren't in an infinite recursion, we check each relationship to see whether we should be following it. If we shouldn't follow it, we simply skip to the next relationship.

PPRecipes/PPRecipes/ExportImportHandler.swift

```
    if relDesc.toMany {
      if let children = mo.valueForKey(name) as? [NSManagedObject] {
        var array = [[String:AnyObject]]()
        for childMO in children {
          array.append(moToDictionary(childMO))
        }
        dict[name] = array
      }
    } else {
      if let childMO = mo.valueForKey(name) as? NSManagedObject {
        dict[name] = moToDictionary(childMO)
      }
    }
  }

  return dict
}
```

When performing this copy, it's easy to accidentally copy the entire Core Data repository. Because all our objects are linked via two-way relationships, if we built a recursive method to copy the objects and follow their relationships, we'd end up with a complete duplicate of all the recipes.

To prevent this, we added a check in each relationship copy. Whenever it follows a relationship, it first checks to make sure that the destination entity should be copied. We do this with a key-value pair in the data model. If there's a key called PPExportRelationship and that key has a value of NO, we skip the relationship. By taking this step, we guarantee the entity tree is copied in only one direction, as shown here.

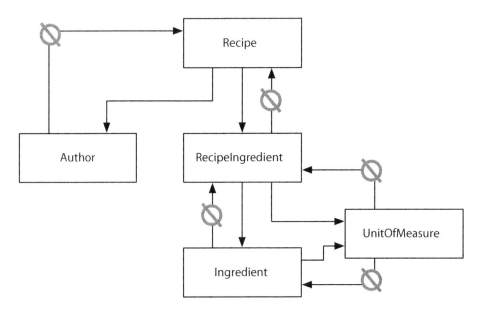

From the perspective of the current NSManagedObject, there are two types of relationships: to-one or to-many. If it's a to-one relationship, we grab the object at the other end of the relationship and turn it into a dictionary for inclusion in our master dictionary.

If the relationship is a to-many, we need to iterate over the resulting set and turn each NSManagedObject into a dictionary and include it in a temporary array. Once we've iterated over all of the objects in the relationship, we add the entire array to our master dictionary using the relationship name as the key.

Once all the relationships have been processed, we return the dictionary to the main() so that we can complete the final step.

PPRecipes/PPRecipes/ExportImportHandler.swift

```
    let json = self.moToDictionary(localRecipe)
    do {
      let d = try NSJSONSerialization.dataWithJSONObject(json, options: [])
      dispatch_async(dispatch_get_main_queue()) {
        self.handler(data: d, error: nil)
      }
    } catch let error as NSError {
      dispatch_async(dispatch_get_main_queue()) {
        self.handler(data: nil, error: error)
      }
    }
  })
}
```

At the end of the main(), we use the NSJSONSerialization class to turn the dictionary structure into a JSON structure. Note that the PPRExportOperation doesn't care if the serialization is successful. It just passes the result and the potential error off to the completion block. It's up to the caller to handle any error in the processing.

Import Operation

The reverse of exporting recipes is to be able to import them. The experience we're looking for is as follows:

1. The user receives a recipe in another application (for example, in Mail).

2. The user taps the recipe, and it opens in our application.

3. Our recipe application receives the data and consumes it.

To accomplish this workflow, we need to step into our UIApplicationDelegate and do a few updates.

PPRecipes/PPRecipes/AppDelegate.swift

```
func application(application: UIApplication, openURL url: NSURL,
  sourceApplication: String?, annotation: AnyObject) -> Bool {
  guard let controller = dataController else {
    fileToOpenURL = url
    return true
  }
  if controller.persistenceInitialized {
    consumeIncomingFileURL(url)
  } else {
    fileToOpenURL = url
  }
  return true
}
```

The first change adds the method application(openURL, sourceApplication, annotation). This method will be called whenever another app is requesting that we open a file. If our application has been running for a while and the Core Data stack is fully initialized, then we can process the file immediately. If the stack isn't fully initialized (for instance, it freshly launched with the opening of the file), then we can store the NSURL and use it once the context has been initialized.

PPRecipes/PPRecipes/AppDelegate.swift

```
func contextInitialized() {
  if let url = self.fileToOpenURL {
    self.consumeIncomingFileURL(url)
  }
}
```

The next change takes place in contextInitialized(). Once the context is fully initialized, we can consume the NSURL that was passed in on the launch. Since we're going to be consuming the NSURL from more than one potential entry point, we abstract away the handling into a consumeIncomingFileURL: method. Thus, contextInitialized just needs to check whether there's an NSURL to consume and hand it off. Because consumeIncomingFileURL: returns a pass or fail, we can add a logic check here to help capture failures during the development.

Building the Operation

The final change is to handle the consumption of the NSURL. We've already defined a method as consumeIncomingFileURL:.

PPRecipes/PPRecipes/AppDelegate.swift

```
func consumeIncomingFileURL(url: NSURL) {
  guard let data = NSData(contentsOfURL: url) else {
    print("No data loaded")
    return
  }
  guard let moc = dataController?.mainContext else {
    fatalError("mainContext is nil")
  }
  let op = PPRImportOperation(data: data, context: moc, handler: {
    (incomingError) in
    if let error = incomingError {
      print("Error importing data: \(error)")
      //Present an error to the user
    } else {
      //Clear visual feedback
    }
  })
```

```
NSOperationQueue.mainQueue().addOperation(op)
//Give visual feedback of the import
}
```

To consume the NSURL, we first load it into an NSData object. We can then pass the NSData instance off to a newly created PPRImportOperation. Once the operation is complete, we'll display something graphically to the user and kick off the operation. The completion closure for the operation checks to see whether there's an error and then reports the error or dismisses the graphical status.

Our PPRImportOperation has a number of similarities to the PPRExportOperation. However, there's also a bit more complexity.

PPRecipes/PPRecipes/ExportImportHandler.swift

```
let type = NSManagedObjectContextConcurrencyType.PrivateQueueConcurrencyType
let localMOC = NSManagedObjectContext(concurrencyType: type)
localMOC.parentContext = parentContext
```

As with our PPRExportOperation, we start off with the main() method. The first thing we want to do in the main() is construct the private NSManagedObjectContext and associate it as a child for the main context.

PPRecipes/PPRecipes/ExportImportHandler.swift

```
localMOC.performBlockAndWait({
  do {
    try self.processRecipeIntoContext(localMOC)

    try localMOC.save()
  } catch {
    fatalError("Failed to import: \(error)")
  }
})
}
```

Consuming the JSON

Once we have the private context constructed, we want to kick off the consumption of the JSON payload. We could just put the code directly in the main() method, but that would cause the method to get overly long and possibly impact maintainability. So, the performBlockAndWait: method will call processRecipeIntoContext: instead and pass in the context. Since the processRecipeIntoContext: method is being called inside the block, it's still on the proper queue and there's no threading violation.

PPRecipes/PPRecipes/ExportImportHandler.swift

```swift
func processRecipeIntoContext(moc: NSManagedObjectContext) throws {
  let json = try NSJSONSerialization.JSONObjectWithData(incomingData,
    options: [])

  guard let entity = NSEntityDescription.entityForName("Recipe",
    inManagedObjectContext: moc) else {
    fatalError("Unable to resolve Recipe")
  }

  switch json {
  case let single as [String:AnyObject]:
    let recipe = NSManagedObject(entity: entity,
      insertIntoManagedObjectContext: moc)
    populateFromDictionary(single, withMO: recipe)
  case let array as [[String:AnyObject]]:
    for recipeJSON in array {
      let recipe = NSManagedObject(entity: entity,
        insertIntoManagedObjectContext: moc)
      populateFromDictionary(recipeJSON, withMO: recipe)
    }
  default: break
  }
}
```

We start the processRecipeIntoContext: method by using the NSJSONSerializer to convert the NSData into a JSON structure. If that conversion fails, we call the completion block and let the operation finish.

Once we have the data in a JSON structure, we must check whether the top-level object is an array or a dictionary. Adding this check makes the import operation more flexible and capable of handling the imported recipes. If the top-level object is a dictionary, we know there's a single recipe being imported and begin the import operation. If the top-level object is an array, we iterate over the array and construct a recipe for each included dictionary.

For each dictionary (whether there are one or many), we construct an NSManagedObject and pass both the dictionary and the NSManagedObject into populateFromDictionary(withMO:).

PPRecipes/PPRecipes/ExportImportHandler.swift

```swift
func populateFromDictionary(incoming: [String: AnyObject],
  withMO object:NSManagedObject) {

  let entity = object.entity
  for (key, _) in entity.attributesByName {
    object.setValue(incoming[key], forKey:key)
  }
```

In the first part of the populateFromDictionary(withMO:), we want to populate all the attributes of the NSManagedObject. The process is the reverse of what we accomplished in the PPRExportOperation. Here are the steps:

1. We iterate over all of the attributes for the entity.

2. We call setValue(forKey:) on the managed object and pass in the value from the dictionary.

PPRecipes/PPRecipes/ExportImportHandler.swift

```swift
guard let moc = object.managedObjectContext else {
  fatalError("No context available")
}
let createChild: (childDict: [String:AnyObject],
  entity:NSEntityDescription,
  moc:NSManagedObjectContext) -> NSManagedObject = {
  (childDict, entity, moc) in
  let destMO = NSManagedObject(entity: entity,
    insertIntoManagedObjectContext: moc)
  self.populateFromDictionary(childDict, withMO: destMO)
  return destMO
}
```

The next step is to create a closure to avoid repeating ourselves later in this method. When dealing with the creation of relationships, we'll create one or more child objects and associate them with the NSManagedObject we're currently working on. Whether we're creating one or many child objects, the steps are virtually identical. We'll use a closure to perform the identical portions of the process and avoid ending up with two copies of that code.

Therefore, the purpose of the closure is to construct the new NSManagedObject and recursively call -populateFromDictionary(withMO:) for the new NSManagedObject. The block makes the rest of this method easier to follow and maintain.

PPRecipes/PPRecipes/ExportImportHandler.swift

```swift
  for (name, relDesc) in entity.relationshipsByName {
    let childStructure = incoming[name]
    if childStructure == nil {
      continue
    }
    guard let destEntity = relDesc.destinationEntity else {
      fatalError("no destination entity assigned")
    }
    if relDesc.toMany {
      guard let childArray = childStructure as? [[String: AnyObject]] else {
        fatalError("To-many relationship with malformed JSON")
      }
      var children = [NSManagedObject]()
```

```
    for child in childArray {
      let mo = createChild(childDict: child, entity: destEntity, moc: moc)
      children.append(mo)
    }
    object.setValue(children, forKey: name)
  } else {
    guard let child = childStructure as? [String: AnyObject] else {
      fatalError("To-many relationship with malformed JSON")
    }
    let mo = createChild(childDict: child, entity: destEntity, moc: moc)
    object.setValue(mo, forKey: name)
  }
}
}
```

With the attributes populated, we now need to populate the relationships. We begin by iterating over the dictionary from the NSEntityDescription that describes all of the relationships of our current NSManagedObject. For each relationship, we check whether any data is available. If there's no data, then there's nothing to process. The iterator returns the key from the dictionary, which is the name of the relationship (and also the name of the accessor).

If there's data to process, we next check whether the relationship is a to-one or a to-many. If it's a to-one, we can invoke our block and create the child NSManagedObject. We can then set the resulting NSManagedObject using setValue(forKey:) and the key from our relationship dictionary.

If the relationship is a to-many, we kick off an iterator to step over the collection and create one NSManagedObject for each dictionary inside the collection.

Once we've walked the entire JSON structure, the final step is to save the local NSManagedObjectContext. That save results in the changes being pushed directly to the main NSManagedObjectContext and the user interface is updated accordingly.

Asynchronous Saving

One of the biggest issues with threading and Core Data has to do with *thread blocking*. No matter how cleverly you write the import and export operations, sooner or later you need to block the main queue to let the main NSManagedObjectContext talk to the NSPersistentStoreCoordinator and save changes out to disk.

Fortunately, this is a solvable problem and requires a small change to the Core Data stack. If you start your Core data stack with a private queue, NSManagedObjectContext, and associate it with the NSPersistentStoreCoordinator, you can have the main NSManagedObjectContext as a child of the private NSManagedObjectContext. Furthermore, when the main NSManagedObjectContext is saved, it won't produce a disk hit and will instead be nearly instantaneous. From there, whenever you want to actually write to disk you can kick off a save on the private contact and get asynchronous saves.

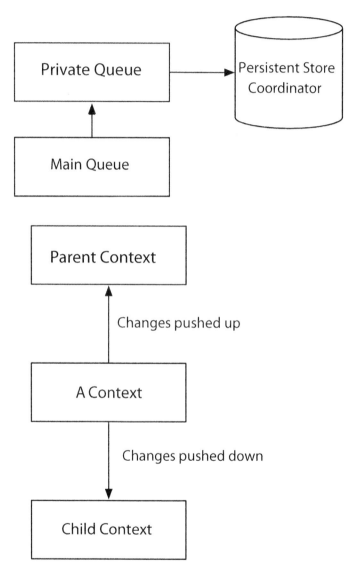

Adding this ability to the application requires a relatively small change. First, you need to add a property to the PPRDataController to hold onto the new private NSManagedObjectContext. Next, you tweak the -initializeCoreDataStack a bit.

```
guard let modelURL = NSBundle.mainBundle().URLForResource("PPRecipes",
  withExtension: "momd") else {
  fatalError("Failed to locate DataModel.momd in app bundle")
}
guard let mom = NSManagedObjectModel(contentsOfURL: modelURL) else {
  fatalError("Failed to initialize MOM")
}
let psc = NSPersistentStoreCoordinator(managedObjectModel: mom)

var type = NSManagedObjectContextConcurrencyType.PrivateQueueConcurrencyType
writerContext = NSManagedObjectContext(concurrencyType: type)
writerContext?.persistentStoreCoordinator = psc

type = NSManagedObjectContextConcurrencyType.MainQueueConcurrencyType
mainContext = NSManagedObjectContext(concurrencyType: type)
mainContext?.parentContext = writerContext
```

Before, we had one NSManagedObjectContext configured to be on the main queue and writing to the NSPersistentStoreCoordinator. Now we have added a new NSManagedObjectContext that's of type NSPrivateQueueConcurrencyType. We also set the NSPersistentStoreCoordinator to that private queue. Finally, we construct our main queue NSManagedObjectContxt. Instead of handing off the NSPersistentStoreCoordinator to the main context, we give it to the parent: the private queue context.

With that change, any saves on the main NSManagedObjectContext will push up the changes only to the private queue NSManagedObjectContext. No writing to the NSPersistentStoreCoordinator occurs. However, there are times when we really do want to write to disk and persist our data changes. In that case, a couple of other changes are in order.

```
func saveContext() {
  guard let main = mainContext else {
    fatalError("save called before mainContext is initialized")
  }
  main.performBlockAndWait({
    if !main.hasChanges { return }
    do {
      try main.save()
    } catch {
      fatalError("Failed to save mainContext: \(error)")
    }
  })
  guard let writer = writerContext else {
    return
  }
  writer.performBlock({
    if !writer.hasChanges { return }
```

```
    do {
      try writer.save()
    } catch {
      fatalError("Failed to save writerContext: \(error)")
    }
  })
}
```

Previously in our saveContext() method, we checked to make sure we had an NSManagedObjectContext and that it had changes. In this new implementation, we first call performBlockAndWait: on the main queue context and, inside that block, check to see if there are any changes. If there are no changes, then the block terminates. If there are changes, we call save() on the main queue context and check for errors.

Once the main queue context has been saved (remember a performBlockAndWait: blocks), we can kick off a save on the private queue context. Since we specifically want this save to be asynchronous, we will call performBlock:. Inside the performBlock: the actions are the same. We check to see if there are any changes and, if there are, we call save() and check for errors.

Because we use performBlock: against the private queue context, the main queue is *not* blocked while data is being written out to disk. The application continues to perform with no delays in the user interface.

Debug Concurrency Checking

One of the issues when dealing with any kind of threading is knowing whether or not you got it right. Threading issues are tricky. Things will work in development, they'll work in testing, and then *every once in a while* they stop working in production. Core Data has suffered from this problem as much as any other framework.

Fortunately, as of iOS 8 and OS X10.10 Core Data now has a solution to the problem: a debug flag that you can turn on that will cause an exception if a Core Data object is accessed from the wrong queue.

This flag can be turned on as a runtime argument and I strongly recommend that it be turned on for the debug configuration on every Core Data project.

To turn it, follow these steps:

1. Edit the schema of your project and select the Run target.

2. Select the Arguments tab.

3. Add -com.apple.CoreData.ConcurrencyDebug 1 to Arguments Passed on Launch.

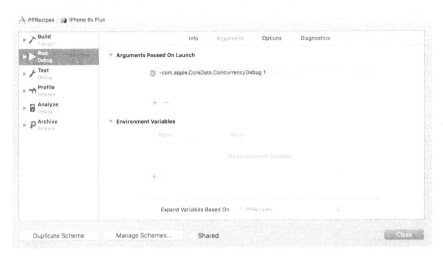

With that flag turned on during debug, the Core Data framework will throw an exception whenever the threading rules of Core Data are violated. If you combine that debug flag with the All Exceptions breakpoint, your application will halt on the exact line of code that's violating the threading rules.

Wrapping Up

Threading is an extremely difficult subject. Very few developers get it right, and even those few still manage to make mistakes in this area. Threading is arguably one of the hardest concepts in computer science.

Threading with Core Data used to be extremely difficult to get right. Now with having only main queue and private queue contexts, it has gotten a lot simpler and it boils down to a simple Boolean decision. If you're working with the UI, then you should be using a main queue context. If you aren't, then you should be using a private queue context.

However, even with this threading model, there are still times when a lot of work needs to be done on the data in a short period of time. For those rare situations, the Core Data framework has two APIs to handle bulk changes to the data structure. They're discussed in the next chapter.

CHAPTER 7

Bulk Changes

Over the years that Core Data has been in production, there have been a few complaints about the framework that struck home and were accurate. Easily the most well-known complaint relates to the ability to change a value in a large number of objects without requiring those objects to all be loaded into memory and then persisted back out to disk. The second largest, most well-known complaint relates to deleting a large number of objects. Again, the desire is to delete a large number of objects without having to load them into memory and then write back out to the persistent store again.

Both of these complaints only apply to the NSSQlite store. Since atomic stores such as the binary store require all of the data to be in memory, there's no issue with doing bulk changes or bulk deletes. But with the SQLite store, either of these changes can be incredibly CPU, disk, and memory intensive.

With the introduction of iOS 8.0 and OS X Yosemite, the first complaint was addressed. With the introduction of iOS 9.0 and OS X El Capitan, the second complaint was addressed.

Running with Scissors

Both of these APIs work by making changes directly on disk. When we utilize either of these APIs, Core Data will construct the appropriate SQL calls and then pass them to SQLite. Nothing gets loaded into memory and therefore the API is executed very quickly, just slightly slower than SQLite itself.

If we can just make changes and/or deletes on disk and avoid having to load them all into memory, why don't we just do that all of the time?

This API comes at a fairly signficiant cost. The changes that we make on disk aren't passed to the NSManagedObjectContext instances in our application.

This means that we can very easily make a change to the data on disk and then our NSManagedObjectContext will try to make a different change and cause issues. When the first API was introduced, the Core Data team likened these APIs to running with scissors. You can do it, but there's greater risk.

First, data validation is performed in memory. When we make a change directly on disk, we're bypassing the validation steps that Core Data normally performs. This means we can break a relationship and have dangling references, we can inject data that's not valid, and so forth. Worse, our application won't notice the issue until it attempts to load the data later and then the user is left in a bad state.

Second, when the changes are made on disk, the version number of the object is updated (as it should be). However, since nothing in memory knows of this change the version number in memory won't match. If Core Data were to attempt to do a save of an object in this state, it'd cause a merge conflict with a potentially negative outcome.

And of course there's the obvious issue. Our user interface won't know about the change and therefore the older data will still be displayed. We can address these issues, but that requires more code on our part. Let's start by looking at a bulk update.

Doing Bulk Updates

Doing a bulk update isn't a common event in most application life cycles. Selecting a large number of emails, or a large number of news items, and marking them as read is a common example of doing a bulk update. While you'll run into these situations, they're unusual and shouldn't be considered a core function of the application. Bulk updates are generally used to get us out of a coding or design "corner."

In our recipes application, we're going to use the bulk update API to change the values of some of our recipes on the first launch after a migration. When we migrate the application to the fourth version, we'll add a Boolean to indicate whether it's a favorite recipe; the default for that recipe is false. Once the migration is complete, we then want to go through all of the recipes and change that default to true for some of them.

First, we want to detect if this change was already made. There are many ways to accomplish this, and we've used other methods in the past. Here, let's use the metadata that's contained with the persistent store to determine if the change has already been processed. This change to the initialization of our Core Data stack determines if we need to do any postmigration processing.

Threading/PPRecipes/PPRDataController.swift

```swift
let queue = dispatch_get_global_queue(DISPATCH_QUEUE_PRIORITY_DEFAULT, 0)
dispatch_async(queue) {
  let fileManager = NSFileManager.defaultManager()
  guard let documentsURL = fileManager.URLsForDirectory(.DocumentDirectory,
    inDomains: .UserDomainMask).first else {
    fatalError("Failed to resolve documents directory")
  }
  let sURL = documentsURL.URLByAppendingPathComponent("PPRecipes.sqlite")
  do {
    let store = try psc.addPersistentStoreWithType(NSSQLiteStoreType,
      configuration: nil, URL: sURL, options: nil)
    if store.metadata[FAVORITE_METADATA_KEY] == nil {
      self.bulkUpdateFavorites()
    }
  } catch {
    fatalError("Failed to initialize PSC: \(error)")
  }
}
```

Every persistent store contains metadata. The metadata resolves to a dictionary that we can query. We can also update this metadata as needed. In this next part of the code, we're looking for a key named FAVORITE_METADATA_KEY. If that key exists, then we know that this particular bit of postprocessing has already been done. If the key is missing, then we need to perform the task.

Threading/PPRecipes/PPRDataController.swift

```swift
func bulkUpdateFavorites() {
  guard let moc = writerContext else {
    fatalError("Writer context is nil")
  }
  moc.performBlock({
    let request = NSBatchUpdateRequest(entityName: "Recipe")
    let aMonthAgo = self.dateFrom1MonthAgo()
    let predicate = NSPredicate(format: "lastUsed >= %@", aMonthAgo)
    request.predicate = predicate
    request.propertiesToUpdate = ["favorite":true]
    request.resultType = .UpdatedObjectIDsResultType
    do {
      guard let result = try moc.executeRequest(request)
        as? NSBatchUpdateResult else {
        fatalError("Unexpected result from executeRequest")
      }
      guard let resultArray = result.result as? [NSManagedObjectID] else {
        fatalError("Unexpected result from batchUpdateResult")
      }
      self.mergeExternalChanges(resultArray, ofType: NSUpdatedObjectsKey)
    } catch {
      fatalError("Failed to execute request: \(error)")
    }
  }
```

The bulkUpdateFavorites method is where we're using the bulk update API. Once we're certain that we're executing on the proper queue for our main NSManagedObjectContext, we start by creating a new NSBatchUpdateRequest. NSBatchUpdateRequest is a subclass of NSPersistentStoreRequest, which is a class that was introduced in OS X 10.7 and iOS 5. An NSBatchUpdateRequest contains all the properties that Core Data needs to execute our update directly on disk. First, we initialize the request with the name of the entity we want to access. We then pass it the predicate to filter the entities that are going to be updated.

In this example, we're going to find all of the recipe entities that have been used in the last month and mark those as favorites. We'll construct a date object that represents one month ago, pass that to the predicate, and then pass the predicate into the NSBatchUpdateRequest.

In addition to the predicate, we need to tell Core Data what properties have to be changed. We do this with a dictionary where the key is the property to change and the value is the new value to apply to the entity. As you can see, we don't have a lot of control over the changes here. There's no logic that we can apply. These are simple, brute-force data changes at the database/persistent store level.

Once we pass the dictionary to the NSBatchUpdateRequest via the propertiesToUpdate, we can define what kind of result we want back. We have three options:

- .StatusOnlyResultType, which won't return anything. If we aren't going to do anything with the response, there's no reason to ask for one.

- .UpdatedObjectIDsResultType, which will give us the NSManagedObjectIDs for each changed entity. If we're going to notify the application of the changes, then we'll want these to do the notification.

- .UpdatedObjectsCountResultType, which will give us a simple count of the number of entities altered.

In this example, we'll walk through updating the user interface of the changes, so we'll ask for the NSManagedObjectID instances back.

Once we have the NSBatchUpdateRequest fully constructed, we can then hand it off to any NSManagedObjectContext we want for processing. In this example, I'm using the writer context because it's closest to the NSPersistentStoreCoordinator. But since this API doesn't notify the NSManagedObjectContext of the change, it really doesn't matter which context we use.

The call to executeRequest returns an AnyObject, and it's up to us to know what the call is giving back to us. Because we set the resultType to .UpdatedObjectIDsResultType, we know that we're going to be getting back an array.

If the call fails, then it will be caught in the do/catch block and handled. As always in the code in this book, we'll treat the error as a fatal condition and crash. How to respond to those errors is a business decision determined by your application's design and requirements.

The call to executeRequest is a blocking call. This means that the call can take a significant amount of time—far less than loading all of the objects into memory, performing the change, and saving them back out to disk, but it will still take time. This is another argument for using the API against the private writer context instead of the context that the user interface is associated with.

Notifying the Application of Changes

Now that we've made changes on disk, we need to notify the contexts of them.

In this example, it's not strictly necessary. Most likely the user interface hasn't touched any of these objects yet. If the objects haven't been loaded into memory, then there's no risk of a conflict. However, it's best that we don't assume they haven't been loaded yet. Users can be very clever.

There are two basic ways to notify our NSManagedObjectContext instances of the changes. We can reset each object individually in each NSManagedObjectContext that it might be associated with, or we can use the new API that was added in iOS 9.0. Let's look at the harder way first.

Manual Object Refreshing

If the situation calls for it, we can instruct each instance of NSManagedObject to refresh individually. This might make sense if we have a view that's observing one specific instance of an entity or we have a user interface that's watching a small subset of objects.

Threading/PPRecipes/PPRDataController.swift

```swift
func manuallyRefreshObjects(objectIDArray: [NSManagedObjectID]) {
  guard let moc = mainContext else {
    fatalError("Unexpected nil context")
  }
  moc.performBlockAndWait({
    for objectID in objectIDArray {
      guard let object = moc.objectRegisteredForID(objectID) else {
        continue
      }
```

```
    if object.fault {
      return
    }
    moc.refreshObject(object, mergeChanges: true)
  }
})
}
```

The manuallyRefreshObjects method accepts an array of NSManagedObjectID instances and walks through that array. Since this method is going to be working with the NSManagedObjectContext that's on the main queue, we want a guarantee that our code will be also executed on the main queue. Therefore, we start by executing the code in a performBlockAndWait to ensure we're on the correct queue.

Inside the block, we iterate over the array of NSManagedObjectID instances and retrieve a reference to the associated NSManagedObject. Note that we're using objectRegisteredForID in this method. objectRegisteredForID will only return a result if the object is registered with the referenced NSManagedObjectContext. If it's not referenced, we certainly don't want to load it, so this method is a perfect fit. From that call, we need to see if we got an object back and that it's not a fault. If it's a fault, we don't need to refresh it because the values aren't in memory.

Once we confirm the NSManagedObject is registered and isn't a fault, we then call refreshObject, which will force the object to reload from the persistent store.

That's a fair amount of work for *each individual NSManagedObject* in the array. Fortunately, there's an easier way.

Remote Notifications

As part of the update for iOS 9.0 and OS X 10.11, the Core Data team gave us a new class method to handle this situation. We can now call mergeChangesFromRemoteContextSave as a class method on NSManagedObjectContext to handle changes that occurred outside our Core Data stack.

The method accepts a dictionary of arrays of NSManagedObjectID instances (either true NSManagedObjectID objects or NSURL representations of them) and also accepts an array of NSManagedObjectContext instances.

As with traditional NSManagedObjectContextDidSaveNotification calls, we can pass in objects that are in three possible states: inserted, updated, and deleted.

Threading/PPRecipes/PPRDataController.swift

```
func mergeExternalChanges(objectIDArray: [NSManagedObjectID],
  ofType type: String) {
  let save = [type: objectIDArray]
```

```
  guard let main = mainContext, let writer = writerContext else {
    fatalError("Unexpected nil context")
  }
  let contexts = [main, writer]
  NSManagedObjectContext.mergeChangesFromRemoteContextSave(save,
    intoContexts: contexts)
}
```

Note in this method that we aren't concerned with what queue things are being executed on. The API call handles that for us. Also note that we're able to update all of the contexts that exist in our application at once.

This method will basically do the same thing that we did in our manual method. But it will handle it for every context we give it and it is faster than our manual method. This is the recommended way to consume remote notifications. With this method our original bulk update call can easily notify the rest of the application of the changes.

Bulk Deletes

The API for handling bulk deletes was added to Core Data after bulk updates. Therefore the API is very similar.

Threading/PPRecipes/PPRDataController.swift

```
func deleteOldRecipes() {
  guard let moc = writerContext else {
    fatalError("Writer context is nil")
  }

  moc.performBlock({
    let yearOld = self.dateFrom1YearAgo()
    let fetch = NSFetchRequest(entityName: "Recipe")
    fetch.predicate = NSPredicate(format: "lastUsed <= %@", yearOld)
    let request = NSBatchDeleteRequest(fetchRequest: fetch)
    request.resultType = .ResultTypeObjectIDs

    do {
      guard let result = try moc.executeRequest(request)
        as? NSBatchDeleteResult else {
        fatalError("Unexpected result from executeRequest")
      }
      guard let resultArray = result.result as? [NSManagedObjectID] else {
        fatalError("Unexpected result from batchDeleteResult")
      }
      self.mergeExternalChanges(resultArray, ofType: NSDeletedObjectsKey)
    } catch {
      fatalError("error performing delete: \(error)")
    }
  })
}
```

The first difference, other than the fact that we're using NSBatchDeleteRequest, is in the initialization of the request. NSBatchDeleteRequest is initialized with an NSFetchRequest rather than an entity name or description. This means we need to build an NSFetchRequest before we can initialize the NSBatchDeleteRequest. I prefer this way as it matches what we're accustomed to with NSFetchedResultsController.

Once the initialization of the NSBatchDeleteRequest is completed, the rest of the implementation is the same. We call executeRequest against an instance of NSManagedObjectContext, which will be a blocking call, and then we can consume the results.

The NSBatchDeleteRequest has the same three types of results as the NSBatchUpdateRequest, so we can choose how to handle the results. Assuming we want to notify the rest of our application that some objects have been deleted, this implementation used the NSBatchDeleteResultTypeObjectIDs and handed off those NSManagedObjectID instances to the mergeExternalChanges method that we used previously.

Things to Consider When Using the Bulk Change APIs

Just because we have these APIs available to us doesn't mean that we should be using them without serious consideration. Several factors impact our decision to use these APIs.

How Fast Is "Faster"?

Doing massive changes to the underlying persistent store will never be instantaneous. No matter what type of database we're working with, this is going to take time. However, compared to the way that we'd "normally" do this type of work with Core Data, these APIs are significantly faster.

Testing against massive persistent stores have shown at least an order of magnitude speed improvement over the traditional way of doing bulk changes. If an operation took nine seconds previously via loading objects into memory and then writing them back out, it'd take less than a second using these bulk operations.

While these APIs don't fall into the realm of a "silver bullet" solution, they're a massive improvement for those rare edge cases when they're needed.

Bad Data

Data validation happens at the object level. Although we still can't shove binary data into a property designed for a number, we can put bad data into the database and it will work.

Worse, if we put bad data into the database, data that would normally fail validation, we won't know that it's bad until the application attempts to both load and then resave that data.

This would be a jarring experience for the user. Imagine loading a recipe, changing the name of it (or just flagging it as being used), and having the application crash or give the user an error saying it's unable to save the recipe.

We need to take care to avoid this potentially very poor user experience. As always, testing rules supreme here.

Merge Conflicts

The one thing that these bulk updates do for us is update the version number of the entity in the persistent store. That version number (that's never exposed to us) is used to determine if something other than the current NSPersistentStore-Coordinator was the last object to write to that entity. This is part of the merge conflict detection system that's a component of Core Data.

If the application later attempts to save that same object and that version number doesn't match, then Core Data will attempt to do a merge. If our merge policy is still set to error, our application will present an error that needs to be handled. If the merge policy causes what's in memory to trump what's on disk, our changes get overwritten.

This can be mitigated fairly easily using the mergeChangesFromRemoteContextSave method that we used in our examples.

No Warnings of Data Changes

This bears repeating. If we don't explicitly tell our application that we changed data on disk, our application won't know about those changes.

If we make our changes before the user interface (or any other part of our application) touches the data, then we're fine. But that's a tightwire act that's just waiting for a fall. Better to use the merge API we discussed and be certain.

Wrapping Up

Ideally we'll never need these APIs. They were added to Core Data to handle those truly edge cases where a requirement came in that was unexpected and the data structure wasn't implemented to handle it.

An API that exists and is rarely used is far better than an API that doesn't exist and is sorely missed. Fortunately for us, these now exist and are not onerous to use.

CHAPTER 8

Network Operations

Over the years, there has been one area of iOS development that has been treated as both difficult and mysterious—so much so that an incredible number of third-party libraries aim at "solving" this difficult and mysterious problem for new developers.

The area that I'm referring to is networking operations. It's extremely rare to see an application available for iOS that doesn't have some form of a network operation inside it.

Fortunately, by using Apple's provided APIs, it's not that difficult to add network operations to an application, and when the application is using Core Data, it becomes even easier.

The Problem and the Approach

The main problem with network operations is time. A network operation will always take some amount of time, and usually the developer wants the user to wait for that network operation to finish before moving on to another task. Users rarely want to wait for an application.

To compound this problem, that amount of time is variable. The developer has no way of knowing if the user is on a fast network or a slow network. Just knowing whether the user is using cellular or Wi-Fi is insufficient. Cellular can be fantastic and Wi-Fi can be terrible.

The basic answer to this problem is that network operations need to be asynchronous. The developer needs to write the networking code in such a way that the network operation can be completed potentially while the user is doing something else.

A better answer is for the application to predict what users are going to need before they need it and fetch that data so that it's ready for the users.

A better solution should allow network operations to be cancelable. If users decide they no longer want the data, then the request should be halted to avoid using battery and bandwidth unnecessarily.

A better solution should be able to prioritize these network requests so that high-priority items can be completed before lower-priority items. Posting a tweet should be treated as a higher-priority item than loading an avatar.

A better solution should keep track of the bandwidth that's being used and aggregate that data over time to determine what bandwidth is and react to the state of the bandwidth that's available.

This better solution involves using subclasses of NSOperation.

The Solution

A network operation is a discrete action and should be coded as such. Therefore, we'll use a subclass of NSOperation as the basis for the network operation.

Instead of using the block-based API provided by Apple, we'll use the delegate functions of NSURLSession to listen to events during the network operation. By implementing the delegate methods, our NSOperation subclass will be integrated into every step of the network request and can make decisions through the operation.

The workflow is as follows:

1. Build the request

2. Start network operation

3. Receive a response from the server

4. Receive N blocks of data from the server

5. Receive a completion delegate callback

6. Process the data

The start() Function

In our NSOperation subclass, we'll handle the first two steps:

PPRecipes/PPRecipes/PPRNetworkOperation.swift

```
class PPRNetworkOperation: NSOperation, NSURLSessionDataDelegate {

  var startTimeInterval: NSTimeInterval?
  var operationRunTime: NSTimeInterval?

  override func start() {
    if cancelled {
      finished = true
      return
    }

    startTimeInterval = NSDate.timeIntervalSinceReferenceDate()

    let url = NSURL(string: "a url to some JSON data")!

    let request = NSMutableURLRequest(URL: url)
    request.HTTPMethod = "POST"

    sessionTask = localURLSession.dataTaskWithRequest(request)
    sessionTask!.resume()
  }
```

In our subclass of NSOperation we also declare that we're implementing the NSURLSessionDataDelegate protocol. Then in the start() function we immediately check to see if it's been canceled. If it has, we abort immediately by indicating we're finished and returning. The NSOperationQueue that's running this operation is watching for the isFinished() variable to change state to determine when the operation is completed. By changing the underlying variable, we can finish the operation before it starts.

Assuming that the operation was not canceled, the next step is to construct the NSURLRequest. An NSURLRequest is an object that describes the request that's going to the server. It can be simple or complicated. If the request needs authorization tokens or parameters for the server, it gets a little more complicated. In this example, the only complication we're adding is setting it to a "POST" request.

Once the NSURLRequest has been constructed, the final step is to create the NSURLSessionDataTask and start it by calling resume().

The Delegate Functions

Once the NSURLSessionDataTask has been started, it will use another thread to make a connection to the server and send our request. The server will then respond with a response code. That code can be an error condition, but normally it's a "request accepted" code that indicates data will be coming. Our NSOperation subclass receives this code in the URLSession(: dataTask: didReceiveResponse: completionHandler:) delegate function.

PPRecipes/PPRecipes/PPRNetworkOperation.swift

```swift
func URLSession(session: NSURLSession, dataTask: NSURLSessionDataTask,
  didReceiveResponse response: NSURLResponse,
  completionHandler: (NSURLSessionResponseDisposition) -> Void) {
    if cancelled {
      finished = true
      sessionTask?.cancel()
      return
    }
    //TODO: Check the response code and react appropriately
    completionHandler(.Allow)
}
```

The URLSession(: dataTask: didReceiveResponse: completionHandler:) function is another opportunity to look for a cancel state and abort the network operation. Assuming that the operation is not canceled, our operation should check the status code and determine whether the operation should proceed. To proceed to receiving data, we need to execute the completionHandler and pass it a NSURLSessionResponseDisposition. The normal disposition is .Allow.

PPRecipes/PPRecipes/PPRNetworkOperation.swift

```swift
func URLSession(session: NSURLSession, dataTask: NSURLSessionDataTask,
  didReceiveData data: NSData) {
    if cancelled {
      finished = true
      sessionTask?.cancel()
      return
    }
    incomingData.appendData(data)
}
```

The next delegate function to be called is NSURLSession(: dataTask: didReceiveData:), which can be called numerous times. The size of the data packet that comes back will vary depending on a large number of factors that are outside our control. In this function there are only two things we need to do: handle a possible cancelation, and store the partial data. By keeping an instance of NSMutableData in our NSOperation subclass, we can easily append the new data and store it, waiting for the NSURLSessionDataTask to finish.

PPRecipes/PPRecipes/PPRNetworkOperation.swift

```swift
func URLSession(session: NSURLSession, task: NSURLSessionTask,
  didCompleteWithError error: NSError?) {
    if cancelled {
      finished = true
      sessionTask?.cancel()
      return
    }
```

```
  if error != nil {
    print("Failed to receive response: \(error)")
    finished = true
    return
  }
  do {
    try processData()
  } catch {
    print("Error processing data: \(error)")
  }
  finished = true
  let end = NSDate.timeIntervalSinceReferenceDate()
  if let startTimeInterval = startTimeInterval {
    operationRunTime = end - startTimeInterval
  }
}
```

The last call we normally get is NSURLSession(: task: didCompleteWithError:), which signals the end of the connection to the server. If this network request completed successfully, the error will be nil; otherwise, we can inspect the error to see what went wrong.

Processing the Data

Once the NSURLSession(: task: didCompleteWithError:) function is called, we can start processing the data that was received. The data is currently in an unusable state (just a block of binary data) and needs to be turned into something we can work with. The first step is to use NSJSONSerialization to turn the data into a usable structure.

PPRecipes/PPRecipes/PPRNetworkOperation.swift

```
func processData() throws {
  if incomingData.length == 0 {
    print("No data received")
    return
  }
  let id = incomingData
  let json = try NSJSONSerialization.JSONObjectWithData(id, options: [])
  guard let collection = json as? [[String: AnyObject]] else {
    fatalError("Unexpected JSON Structure: \(json)")
  }
```

The processData() function is set up to throw if there's an error. If the conversion of the data to objects produces an error, it will bubble up to the calling method, which will process the error.

Once the data has been converted into an object structure, we can start processing it and storing the data in Core Data. Since all NSOperation instances run on non-main queues, it's safe to assume that directly using the main queue NSManagedObjectContext would violate the threading rules of Core Data. Therefore, the next step is to construct a private queue context and use that context to store the data received.

PPRecipes/PPRecipes/PPRNetworkOperation.swift

```
let t = NSManagedObjectContextConcurrencyType.PrivateQueueConcurrencyType
let moc = NSManagedObjectContext(concurrencyType: t)
moc.parentContext = managedObjectContext

moc.performBlockAndWait {
  for jsonObject in collection {
    self.constructRecipeFromJSON(jsonObject, moc: moc)
  }
}

moc.performBlockAndWait {
  do {
    try moc.save()
  } catch {
    fatalError("Failed to save child context: \(error)")
  }
}
}
```

Since we required a valid NSManagedObjectContext when this NSOperation subclass was created, we'll use that passed-in NSManagedObjectContext as the parent to the context we're creating locally. Once the local NSManagedObjectContext has been created, we can start iterating over the received data, constructing recipes from it, and storing them in the local context.

Once all of the incoming objects have been consumed and stored in the local context, we can save the local context. Doing so will push those changes up to the parent context, and the operation can finish.

Updating the User Interface

You'll notice that we didn't make any calls to the user interface in this network operation. The reason is that Core Data handles it for us. When we push the changes from the local NSManagedObjectContext to the main NSManagedObjectContext via the call to save(), the main NSManagedObjectContext will automatically update all its listeners.

Because our user interface is using NSFetchedResultsController instances, those NSFetchedResultsController instances will get delegate callbacks as part of the save, notifying them of the new recipe objects and causing the user interface to be updated.

By designing our network operations in this manner, we avoid tight coupling between the network calls and the user interface. This in turn leads to better maintainability of the codebase.

Monitoring Bandwidth

The monitoring of bandwidth is a useful feature. Depending on the needs of an application, it can be extremely useful to know if the user is currently in a low- or a high-bandwidth situation. Decisions on what data and how much data to download can be made once the amount of available bandwidth is known.

When we're using NSOperation subclasses for our network calls, we can aggregate the data from each operation to determine bandwidth. To start with, we add a variable to each operation:

```
var startTimeInterval: NSTimeInterval?
```

Then in the start() function we track when the operation started:

```
startTimeInterval = NSDate.timeIntervalSinceReferenceDate()
```

Finally, in the NSURLSession(: task: didCompleteWithError:) function, we calculate how long the operation took:

```
let end = NSDate.timeIntervalSinceReferenceDate()
operationRunTime = end - startTimeInterval
```

Now the operation has the information it needs to aggregate bandwidth. To utilize this information, the caller of the operation would add a completion block to the operation instance:

```
let moc = self.managedObjectContext
let operation = PPRNetworkOperation(moc)
operation.completionBlock = {
  let length = operation.incomingData.length
  let duration = operation.operationRunTime
  self.aggregateNetworkCall(length: length, duration: duration)
}
```

The aggregateNetworkCall(length: duration:) can use any system that makes sense to the business needs of the application. It can be as simple as a small state machine (good vs. bad) that swings back and forth between states depending on the results from the network operation.

Once the application knows how good the bandwidth is, it can make some simple decisions based on that information:

- If the bandwidth is bad, nonvital images don't get loaded.

- If the bandwidth is good, nonvital data gets loaded that would otherwise wait until it's specifically requested.

- If the bandwidth changes from good to bad, nonvital network operations can be suspended or canceled until the bandwidth returns to a good state.

And many other decisions... With the combination of real-time bandwidth information and NSOperation subclasses, it becomes very straightforward to make and manage these decisions.

Handling Priorities

As part of the NSOperation and NSOperationQueue API, we can assign priorities to operations as well as make one operation dependent on another. By doing so, we can control what operations get performed first and which ones get performed later or perhaps never. Business decisions play a large part in deciding these priorities, but generally when the user is creating data and sending it out to the network, that should take priority over receiving data.

Canceling Operations

When data is no longer needed, the network operation associated with it should be canceled. This makes the application a good citizen on the system as well as saving battery life and increasing application performance.

If a user leaves a scene that was requesting a large amount of data, perhaps stopping a video early or leaving a view before the image loads, the network request should be canceled. With NSOperation subclasses, we can cancel a network operation that's no longer needed.

In addition to those logical cancelations, there's the situation of the user leaving the application. We're notified when the user exits the application and we're given an opportunity to clean up before being suspended.

Our application should be using that time to shut down unnecessary network operations and potentially asking for additional time if a critical network operation is still in process. At the time of application termination (or entering the background), we can inspect what's left in the NSOperationQueue and decide if more time is required, or shut down the operations that don't need to finish.

Accessing the Network Operations

The last question to be answered is where to keep these NSOperation subclasses. Ideally they should be created, accessed, and referenced from a central location. The AppDelegate could be used, but the AppDelegate tends to turn into a bit of a dumping ground. A superior location would be in the DataController since the network operations have a close tie with Core Data. In addition, since the DataController is being passed through the view controllers already, it's a small change to include convenience methods to kick off network operations and let the DataController house the NSOperationQueue that runs the operations.

Wrapping Up

By utilizing NSOperation instances for our network operations, we can build small, discrete units of work that become easy to manage. By combining those NSOperation subclasses with Core Data, we have access to loosely coupled units of work that can update the user interface asynchronously.

CHAPTER 9

Using Core Data with iCloud

Starting with iOS 5.0 and Mac OS X 10.7 Lion, Apple has added the ability to sync a Core Data application to iCloud. For developers, that means we can easily add cloud sharing of our application's data without the need to build our own servers. It also means our applications can share data between devices and computers.

iCloud integration allows developers to sync data between any number of computers and devices; we can sync between an iPhone application, an iPad application, a Mac application, or any combination thereof. In fact, we can add the ability to sync with our very first application, and new clients added later will automatically sync once we make them available to our users.

There are two approaches to adding iCloud integration to a Core Data application on iOS. We can just add a few options to our NSPersistentStore, or we can use the new API called UIManagedDocument. Currently, on OS X, we don't have a full counterpart to UIManagedDocument and therefore we only have one option for iCloud integration, which will be discussed later in this chapter.

If we have an existing application, the choice is simple: adding the options to the NSPersistentStore has the smallest impact on our codebase. However, in order to properly move everything into iCloud, we do need to perform some additional work, as outlined in *Migrating an Existing Application*, on page 135. For a new application, it's worth looking at UIManagedDocument and deciding whether it makes sense for the particular type of application you're designing. Once the choice between using a UIManagedDocument or a standard Core Data stack has been made, the behavior of iCloud is the same. Therefore, we're going to start by examining UIManagedDocument and then look at wiring iCloud into a standard stack. Once we're past those differences, we'll take a deeper dive into the other details of using iCloud.

Introducing the UIManagedDocument

With the introduction of iCloud, Apple introduced a new API called UIDocument. UIDocument is designed to be an abstract parent class that makes it easy to integrate applications with iCloud. One of the Core Data API changes for iOS 6.0 is UIManagedDocument, a subclass of UIDocument.

Fundamentally, the biggest advantage of using UIManagedDocument is the ability to abstract away the saving and state of your Core Data stack. With UIManaged-Document, saving is handled automatically and generally occurs asynchronously. You can request saves to occur more frequently than the autosave handles, but in general you shouldn't need to do that. In addition to managing the saving of the Core Data stack, UIManagedDocument has added features that allow you to store files outside of the persistent store that will also be pushed to iCloud.

UIManagedDocument is meant to be used in applications that have a document design. Pages, Numbers, Omnigraffle, and so on are great examples of iOS applications that manage a form of document. Having said that, however, there's nothing stopping you from using a UIManagedDocument as your single Core Data stack enclosure. It's not specifically designed for a single stack design, but it will work. It's even appealing in some ways, since it abstracts out the creation of the stack.

iCloud/PPRecipes/PPRDataController.swift

```swift
let queue = dispatch_get_global_queue(DISPATCH_QUEUE_PRIORITY_DEFAULT, 0)

dispatch_async(queue) {
  let fileManager = NSFileManager.defaultManager()
  guard let documentsURL = fileManager.URLsForDirectory(.DocumentDirectory,
    inDomains: .UserDomainMask).first else {
    fatalError("Failed to resolve documents directory")
  }
  let storeURL = documentsURL.URLByAppendingPathComponent("PPRecipes")
```

The first step in constructing a UIManagedDocument is to resolve the file URL where we will store the document and determine what the file URL is going to be for iCloud. This first step, configuring where we're saving the data, is virtually the same as when we construct a standard Core Data stack. We determine where the documents directory is located via a call to the NSFileManager, and then we append a path component to the end to identify our document. In this case, the document is called PPRecipes.

The second URL—the iCloud URL—is a bit different. -URLForUbiquityContainerIdentifier: is a new addition to the NSFileManager that came with iCloud. This call requests a URL in which to store information that iCloud is going to use to sync the NSPersistentStore. If iCloud is disabled on the device (iOS or OS X), this call returns nil. Once we have a URL and it's not nil, we know iCloud is available, and we need to configure it.

It's the second call that has an interesting issue; specifically, this call can take an indeterminate amount of time. If iCloud isn't available or if the directory structure had previously been constructed, this call could return nearly instantaneously. However, if iCloud is enabled and the directory structure needs to be constructed, the call might take a significant amount of time—long enough that we need to worry about the watchdog killing it for taking too long to launch. Therefore, because of this method call, we need to wrap all of this construction in a dispatch queue and let it run asynchronously with the main thread.

Once we know whether iCloud is available, we can continue our configuration.

Configuring iCloud

To add iCloud to a Core Data stack, we need to add more options to the NSPersistentStore when we add the NSPersistentStore to the NSPersistentStoreCoordinator.

iCloud/PPRecipes/PPRDataController.swift

```
var options = [String:AnyObject]()
options[NSMigratePersistentStoresAutomaticallyOption] = true
options[NSInferMappingModelAutomaticallyOption] = true

if let cloudURL = fileManager.URLForUbiquityContainerIdentifier(nil) {
  let url = cloudURL.URLByAppendingPathComponent("PPRecipes")
  let identifier = NSBundle.mainBundle().bundleIdentifier
  options[NSPersistentStoreUbiquitousContentNameKey] = identifier
  options[NSPersistentStoreUbiquitousContentURLKey] = url
}
```

The first part of this code should be familiar. We create an NSMutableDictionary and add the options both to infer a mapping model and to attempt a migration automatically. From there, if iCloud is enabled, we need to add the iCloud URL to our options dictionary. However, we don't want our document stored at the root of our iCloud sandbox. Rather, we want to create a directory under the root with the same name as the document we're creating locally. Therefore, we're going to append "PPRecipes" to the end of the URL. Once the URL is defined, we need to add it to our options dictionary with the key NSPersistentStoreUbiquitousContentURLKey.

In addition to the URL for the storage location, we need to tell iCloud what data it's going to sync. If we have a single application shared between iPhone and iPad, as in our current example, we can use the bundle identifier as a unique key to define what data is to be shared across the devices. However, if we're also sharing data with a desktop application, the bundle identifier may not be appropriate. The data identifier is stored in the options dictionary with the key NSPersistentStoreUbiquitousContentNameKey.

The addition of these two keys is the bare minimum required to enable iCloud for an iOS application. With that information, the operating system creates a directory for the content, downloads any content that exists in the cloud, and begins syncing the data. However, as with the URL call, the initial download (or for that matter subsequent syncing) can take an indeterminate amount of time. If there's nothing currently in the store, the creation of the directory structure will be virtually instantaneous. But if there's data to download, it could take some time, depending on the speed of the network connection and the amount of data. Therefore, the application needs to be able to handle a delay in the creation of the persistent store. There are many ways to deal with this delay, and that's an exercise left to the user experience experts; handling the blending of synchronous and asynchronous actions is always a problem to be dealt with as part of the user experience.

Building the UIManagedDocument

Once the options dictionary has been constructed, it's time to build the UIManagedDocument.

iCloud/PPRecipes/PPRDataController.swift

```swift
let document = UIManagedDocument(fileURL: storeURL)
document.persistentStoreOptions = options

let type = NSMergePolicyType.MergeByPropertyObjectTrumpMergePolicyType
let policy = NSMergePolicy(mergeType: type)
document.managedObjectContext.mergePolicy = policy

let completion: (Bool) -> Void = { (success:Bool) -> Void in
  if !success {
    print("Failed to open file: \(storeURL)")
    return
  }

  if let closure = self.initializationComplete {
    dispatch_async(dispatch_get_main_queue()) {
      closure()
    }
  }
}

self.managedDocument = document

guard let path = storeURL.path else {fatalError("Unable to resolve path")}
```

```
if NSFileManager.defaultManager().fileExistsAtPath(path) {
  document.openWithCompletionHandler(completion)
} else {
  document.saveToURL(storeURL, forSaveOperation: .ForCreating,
    completionHandler: completion)
}
```

Constructing the UIManagedDocument is a case of calling the initializer fileURL: and passing in the storeURL that we previously constructed. Once the UIManagedDocument is initialized, we can set the options for the NSPersistentStore via a call to persistentStoreOptions variable. Note that we don't have the ability to add more than one NSPersistentStore to a UIManagedDocument.

We also want to take this opportunity to set the merge policy for the UIManagedDocument. This setting is performed on the NSManagedObjectContext directly.

Unlike when we construct a straight Core Data stack, though, the initialization of the UIManagedDocument isn't the end for us. We must now save it. We could save it later, but it's best to put all of this initialization code in the same place rather than have it spread out. To save the UIManagedDocument, we must first discover if it already exists; based on that information, we can call the appropriate method.

Whether the UIManagedDocument existed before, the process is the same: we call a method on the UIManagedDocument and pass in a completion handler. Since that completion handler is the same no matter which method we call, construct the completion handler first and then determine which method to call.

In the completion handler, we check to see whether it completed successfully. If it wasn't successful, we present an error to the user and perhaps try to recover from the error. If the completion was successful, we want to notify the AppDelegate that the UIManagedDocument has been initialized and that normal program flow can resume.

With the completion block constructed, we can now ask the NSFileManager if the file already exists; if it does, we call openWithCompletionHandler() on the UIManagedDocument. If it doesn't exist, we need to create it with a call to saveToURL(: forSaveOperation:completionHandler:). If this seems overly complicated, that's because it is. This really should be abstracted away into the framework.

Observing Changes to the UIManagedDocument

Once our UIManagedDocument has been constructed, it can be quite useful to know its current state. Since the UIManagedDocument saves on its own accord, we won't automatically know whether it's clean or dirty. We need some kind of callback system in place to notify us. Fortunately, the UIManagedDocument does broadcast notifications when the state changes. By adding our PPRData-Controller as an observer to the notification UIDocumentStateChangedNotification, we're notified of those changes and can act accordingly.

iCloud/PPRecipes/PPRDataController.swift

```swift
let center = NSNotificationCenter.defaultCenter()
center.addObserver(self,
  selector: #selector(PPRDataController.documentStateChanged(_:)),
  name: UIDocumentStateChangedNotification, object: document)
```

There are several places that we could start observing this notification; placing it in the initializeDocument() is a personal preference. When this notification fires, we receive the UIManagedDocument as the object of the notification. From the UIManagedDocument, we then respond accordingly.

iCloud/PPRecipes/PPRDataController.swift

```swift
func documentStateChanged(notification: NSNotification) {
  guard let doc = notification.object as? UIManagedDocument else {
    fatalError("Unexpected object in notification")
  }
  switch doc.documentState {
  case UIDocumentState.Normal:
    print("UIDocumentStateNormal: \(notification)")
  case UIDocumentState.Closed:
    print("UIDocumentStateClosed: \(notification)")
  case UIDocumentState.InConflict:
    print("UIDocumentStateInConflict: \(notification)")
  case UIDocumentState.SavingError:
    print("UIDocumentStateSavingError: \(notification)")
  case UIDocumentState.EditingDisabled:
    print("UIDocumentStateDisabled: \(notification)")
  case UIDocumentState.ProgressAvailable:
    print("UIDocumentStateProgressAvailable: \(notification)")
  default: break
  }
}
```

From the state of the UIManagedDocument, we can update our user interface to reflect that state and tell the user what's going on with the underlying data.

Manually Saving a UIManagedDocument

By default, the UIManagedDocument works to ensure that our data is saved as frequently as makes sense. The UIDocument design knows to listen for UIApplicationWillResignActiveNotification, UIApplicationDidEnterBackgroundNotification, and UIApplicationWillTerminateNotification notifications. When it receives one of these notifications, it saves. It also saves periodically during the life of the application. On average, these periodical saves take place every five minutes.

However, we know our application better than the frameworks do. We know when something nonrecoverable or vital has just occurred, and we can decide that a save is mandatory at a specific point. Fortunately, it's possible to convey that need to UIManagedDocument.

iCloud/PPRecipes/PPRDataController.swift

```
guard let fileURL = managedDocument?.fileURL else {
  fatalError("document did not have a URL")
}
managedDocument?.saveToURL(fileURL, forSaveOperation: .ForOverwriting,
  completionHandler: { (success) in
    //Handle failure
})
```

The call to request a save is the same we used when we were initially creating the UIManagedDocument. Further, we can request the URL for the save directly from the UIManagedDocument. The only detail left is planning how to properly respond to a failed save.

Direct NSManagedObjectContext to iCloud

If you've been using Core Data for a while, you'll feel right at home creating a Core Data stack; otherwise, this code will look similar to the stack we discussed in Chapter 2, *Under the Hood*, on page 13. The code to add iCloud to the Core Data stack is short, straightforward, and easy to add. This is good and bad. It's good, in that it takes a small amount of effort to add iCloud to your Core Data–based application, but it's bad because there aren't very many options to configure, and it's a one-size-fits-all design. If your data model is complex or if you have elements that you don't want to sync, then lack of configurability will cause some interesting solutions. For example, if you have nonsyncable data, then you may need to split your data into more than one persistent store. Another situation that can feel limiting is if you have a high churn rate in your data structures. iCloud prefers to have an opportunity to process the data, and a high rate of content creation or change can cause it to get backed up. In that situation, it may be necessary to "roll up" your data changes to decrease the number of entities being created or the frequency of saves. Reviewing your application's activities in instruments (as discussed in Chapter 5, *Performance Tuning*, on page 65) will help you to determine whether you've strayed off the golden path.

Configuring iCloud

To integrate iCloud with our Core Data stack, we insert some additional options to the NSPersistentStore when we add the NSPersistentStore to the NSPersistentStoreCoordinator.

iCloud/PPRecipes/PPRDataController.swift

```
var options = [String:AnyObject]()
options[NSMigratePersistentStoresAutomaticallyOption] = true
options[NSInferMappingModelAutomaticallyOption] = true

if let cloudURL = fileManager.URLForUbiquityContainerIdentifier(nil) {
  let url = cloudURL.URLByAppendingPathComponent("PPRecipes")
  let identifier = NSBundle.mainBundle().bundleIdentifier
  options[NSPersistentStoreUbiquitousContentNameKey] = identifier
  options[NSPersistentStoreUbiquitousContentURLKey] = url
}
```

The first part of this code should be familiar. We create a dictionary and add the options both to infer a mapping model and to attempt a migration automatically. From here, though, we're in new territory. URLForUbiquityContainerIdentifier() is a new addition to the NSFileManager that came with iCloud. This call requests an NSURL used to store information that iCloud is going to use to sync the NSPersistentStore. If iCloud is disabled on this device (or Mac OS X computer), this call will return nil. Once we have the NSURL and have established that it's not nil, we know iCloud is available, and can begin to configure it.

The URL we receive points to a file path; it looks something like this:

```
file://localhost/private/var/mobile/Library/
Mobile%20Documents/K7T84T27W4~com~pragprog~PPRecipes/
```

Notice this file path is outside our application sandbox. Even so, we have some control over what goes into this directory. For example, if we use a document-based application, we could append the name of the document onto this path so that each document is kept separate. In our current example, however, we're going to create a single subdirectory for our Core Data stack. This will help us in the future if we decide to make changes or sync additional items. Once the URL is defined, we need to add it to our options dictionary with the key NSPersistentStoreUbiquitousContentURLKey.

In addition to the URL for the storage location, we must tell iCloud what data it should be syncing with. If we have a single application shared between iPhone and iPad, as in our current example, we can use the bundle identifier as a unique key to define what data is to be shared across the devices. However, if we're also sharing data with a desktop application, the bundle identifier may not be appropriate. The data identifier is stored in the options dictionary with the key NSPersistentStoreUbiquitousContentNameKey.

Once again, the addition of those two keys is the bare minimum required to enable iCloud for an iOS application. With that information, the operating system creates a directory for the content, downloads any content that exists in the cloud, and starts syncing that data for us. However, that initial download (or for that matter subsequent syncing) can take an indeterminate amount of time. If there's nothing currently in the store, the creation of the directory structure will be virtually instantaneous. However, if there's data to download, it could take some time, depending on the speed of the network connection and the amount of data. As before, we must change how we add the NSPersistentStore to the NSPersistentStoreCoordinator.

Asynchronously Adding the NSPersistentStore

Prior to iOS 6.0 and Mac OS X Lion, we could add the NSPersistentStore to the NSPersistentStoreCoordinator directly on the main thread. While this was rarely recommended, it was extremely common. With the addition of iCloud, it's really no longer an option. The process of configuring iCloud happens when we add the NSPersistentStore to the NSPersistentStoreCoordinator, and it happens before the call returns. If iCloud needs to download data and that download takes several seconds, our application will be unresponsive while the download occurs, and our application could be potentially killed from the operating system watchdog for taking too long to start up.

Currently, the best solution to this problem is to add the NSPersistentStore to the NSPersistentStoreCoordinator on a background thread. We can use dispatch queues and blocks to make this relatively painless.

iCloud/PPRecipes/PPRDataController.swift

```
dispatch_async(queue) {
  let fileManager = NSFileManager.defaultManager()
  guard let docURL = fileManager.URLsForDirectory(.DocumentDirectory,
    inDomains: .UserDomainMask).first else {
    fatalError("Failed to resolve documents directory")
  }
  let storeURL = docURL.URLByAppendingPathComponent("PPRecipes.sqlite")
  do {
    try psc.addPersistentStoreWithType(NSSQLiteStoreType,
      configuration: nil, URL: storeURL, options: nil)
  } catch {
    fatalError("Failed to initialize PSC: \(error)")
  }
  self.populateTypeEntities()
  self.persistenceInitialized = true
```

```
if let closure = self.initializationComplete {
  dispatch_async(dispatch_get_main_queue()) {
    closure()
  }
}
```

In this code block, we define the path for our SQLite file and gain a reference to the NSPersistentStoreCoordinator. From there, we add the NSPersistentStore to the NSPersistentStoreCoordinator. Assuming that's successful, we push another block back to the main queue and inform the application that the Core Data stack has been completed and is ready for use.

Once we've completed the construction of the NSPersistentStoreCoordinator, we want to be on the main thread (aka the UI Thread) when we call contextInitialized so that the rest of the AppDelegate initialization doesn't need to dance with threads. Keeping all of the thread jumping in one place makes it easier to maintain.

Consuming Changes from iCloud

Whether we're using a standard Core Data stack or a UIManagedDocument, we need to know when changes come in from iCloud. Changes will always come in asynchronously, and our NSManagedObjectContext won't know about them. It's our responsibility to notify our NSManagedObjectContext of incoming changes. To do that, we need to listen for the change notification via the NSNotificationCenter.

iCloud/PPRecipes/PPRDataController.swift

```
let name = NSPersistentStoreDidImportUbiquitousContentChangesNotification
let center = NSNotificationCenter.defaultCenter()
center.addObserver(self, selector: #selector(mergePSCChanges(_:)),
                   name: name, object: mainContext)
```

Just like with the UIDocumentStateChangedNotification for the UIManagedDocument, it's a good idea to start listening for the NSPersistentStoreDidImportUbiquitousContentChanges-Notification notifications after the Core Data stack (or UIManagedDocument) has been constructed. Therefore, we put the addObserver(: selector: name: object:) call at the end of the initializeCoreDataStack() method in the PPRDataController.

When the notification fires, it can be treated exactly as if a notification from an NSManagedObjectContext is coming in from another thread, as discussed in Chapter 6, *Threading*, on page 79. Although the notification doesn't contain actual NSManagedObject instances, it does contain NSManagedObjectID instances, and the NSManagedObjectContext knows how to consume them as well.

iCloud/PPRecipes/PPRDataController.swift

```swift
func mergePSCChanges(notification: NSNotification) {
  guard let moc = self.mainContext else {
    fatalError("Unexpected nil MOC")
  }
  moc.performBlock() {
    moc.mergeChangesFromContextDidSaveNotification(notification)
  }
}
```

Under the Hood

Now that we've looked at how to integrate iCloud into our Core Data–based application, it's helpful to understand exactly how it works under the hood.

Debug Output

Core Data has several logging levels that we can turn on to watch all of the SQL calls that are generated during an application's life cycle. There are currently three levels to this debugging log, with level 1 being the least chatty and level 3 being the most chatty. We can set this debug output by adding the runtime parameter com.apple.CoreData.SQLDebug to our application and pass along with it the level we want to be set.

In addition to the Core Data debug setting, we can turn on an additional setting to watch all of the chatter *between* Core Data and iCloud. That additional setting is com.apple.coredata.ubiquity.logLevel. For an unknown reason, this logging code responds only to level 3, as shown in the following screenshot on page 134.

Looking at these logs, we can see there's a tremendous amount of activity going on behind the scenes. We can also examine the frequency with which Core Data starts a sync with iCloud and use that information when we're determining how often to generate saves from our application.

Transaction Logs

iCloud functions through transaction logs. Similar to how modern version control systems work, every time a save is performed by an "iCloud-backed" persistent store, a transaction log is created that details what happened in that save. These transaction logs are kept in order and pushed up to the cloud. On other devices, the transaction logs are received and played back onto the receiving persistent store. Through this process, each persistent store is kept in sync with the other. In addition, new persistent stores can be

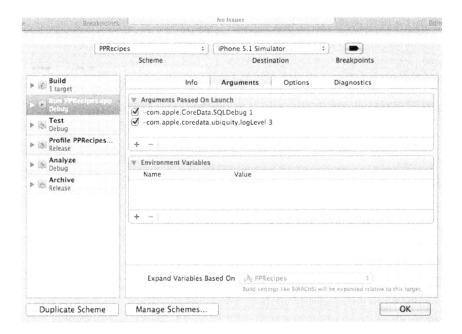

added to the mix by simply starting with an empty store and playing back the transactions one at a time until the new store is brought up-to-date.

If the application has seen a lot of activity, there can be a large number of transaction logs. The large number of transaction logs means any new device must take a significant amount of time to "catch up" with the current state of the persistent store. For this reason, Core Data cuts a new "baseline" on a regular interval. A baseline is effectively a "roll-up" of the transaction logs to a certain point. Any logs after the baseline point will pile up as before. A new store coming into the sync starts with a baseline instead of an empty database and consumes any transaction logs generated after the baseline. This strategy keeps the amount of time it takes to bring a new persistent store up to speed to a minimum.

Turning Off iCloud

Currently, there's an outstanding issue when the user turns off iCloud. When this event occurs, our application receives no notification. The data simply goes away. Some developers have been successful in adding a "sentinel" file to the ubiquitous container (via the URL that gets resolved when we configure iCloud) and monitoring that file. If the file goes away, then we can decide how to handle the state change. Creating a sentinel file hasn't been approved (or disallowed) by Apple, and it may not work in future versions of Core Data.

Ordered Relationships Are Not Allowed

If we integrate iCloud into our application, we can't use the new ordered relationships that were added as of iOS 6.0 and OS X 10.8. iCloud integration does *not* work with ordered relationships. Ideally, this deficiency will be corrected at some point.

Handling Data Migration

A potential issue and surprise with iCloud integration is that only lightweight migration can be used in an iCloud-integrated Core Data application. Heavyweight migration (as in a migration that requires a mapping model) can't be used if iCloud is enabled. With an iCloud-enabled `NSPersistentStore`, the mapping model will simply be ignored, and the migration fails. Therefore, particular care must be taken when you're doing a migration to avoid crossing the limit of lightweight/inferred migration.

If a migration requires more complexity than a lightweight migration can handle, I recommend that you set up a new ubiquitous container and do the migration with iCloud turned off, and then load the data into the new container. To accomplish this, you'd need to follow a procedure similar to the one discussed next.

Migrating an Existing Application

Because Core Data keeps track of changes via transaction logs, it's impossible to just "turn on" iCloud in an existing application and expect all the data to get pushed into the cloud. A few other steps are necessary.

The first question when adding iCloud to an existing iOS application is whether the migration is necessary. There are two key criteria for answering this question:

- Is there any existing data to migrate?
- Has the migration already been performed?

Both of these questions can be answered easily if we do a simple filename change. For example, if our application has always used a SQLite file named PPRecipes.sqlite, then when we want to add iCloud integration to our application, we should start using a filename of PPRecipes-iCloud.sqlite. A simple "does this file exist?" check tells us whether we need to migrate our existing data.

If it's not possible or reasonable to rename the file, the fallback option is to store a flag in the `NSUserDefaults` to let us know whether the migration has occurred. This option is second best for a couple of reasons.

- As we'll demonstrate in a moment, the file needs to be moved anyway.
- NSUserDefaults classes tend to be a bit unreliable, especially during testing.

Assuming we're going to use a file rename strategy to determine whether a migration is required, the first step is to look for the "old" filename to determine whether a migration is required. As part of this change to handle the migration, we're going to refactor the NSPersistentStoreCoordinator initialization code somewhat to make it more maintainable with these additions.

iCloud/PPRecipes/PPRDataController.swift

```swift
let queue = dispatch_get_global_queue(DISPATCH_QUEUE_PRIORITY_DEFAULT, 0)
dispatch_async(queue) {
  let fileManager = NSFileManager.defaultManager()
  guard let docURL = fileManager.URLsForDirectory(.DocumentDirectory,
    inDomains: .UserDomainMask).first else {
      fatalError("Failed to resolve documents directory")
  }

  var options = [String:AnyObject]()
  options[NSMigratePersistentStoresAutomaticallyOption] = true
  options[NSInferMappingModelAutomaticallyOption] = true

  let aCloudURL = fileManager.URLForUbiquityContainerIdentifier(nil)
```

We start the changes at the top of the asynchronous dispatch queue. Notice that we are setting the "universal" options only for the NSPersistentStore at this point. This allows us to reuse the dictionary no matter what path we end up taking. Finally, we request the cloudURL from the NSFileManager so that we can start to determine how to add the NSPersistentStore to the NSPersistentStoreCoordinator.

Now we're ready to make our first decision: is iCloud available or not?

iCloud/PPRecipes/PPRDataController.swift

```swift
guard let cloudURL = aCloudURL else {
  let storeURL = docURL.URLByAppendingPathComponent("PPRecipes.sqlite")
  do {
    try psc.addPersistentStoreWithType(NSSQLiteStoreType,
      configuration: nil, URL: storeURL, options: options)
  } catch {
    fatalError("Failed to initialize PSC: \(error)")
  }
  if let closure = self.initializationComplete {
    dispatch_async(dispatch_get_main_queue()) {
      closure()
    }
  }
  return
}
```

Now that we've added the migration code for iCloud, it's actually the shorter path when iCloud isn't enabled. Therefore, we're going to respond to that decision first. If iCloud isn't available, we resolve the path for the file named PPRecipes.sqlite and add it to the persistent store. If the file doesn't exist, Core Data will create it. This is the traditional logic path.

Once the NSPersistentStore is added to the NSPersistentStoreCoordinator, we check to make sure it was successful and then notify our UIApplicationDelegate that the stack initialization is complete and return. It should be noted that it's possible for the user to turn iCloud back *off* and be fully robust. We should check to see whether that situation occurred. If it did, we must migrate back off of iCloud. That decision branch is left as an exercise for the reader.

iCloud/PPRecipes/PPRDataController.swift

```swift
let filename = "PPRecipes-iCloud.sqlite"
let storeURL = docURL.URLByAppendingPathComponent(filename)
let oldURL = docURL.URLByAppendingPathComponent("PPRecipes.sqlite")
guard let oldURLPath = oldURL.path else {
  fatalError("Unable to resolve path associated with NSURL")
}
var store: NSPersistentStore? = nil
if fileManager.fileExistsAtPath(oldURLPath) {
  do {
    store = try psc.addPersistentStoreWithType(NSSQLiteStoreType,
      configuration: nil, URL: oldURL, options: options)
  } catch {
    fatalError("Error adding store to PSC:\(error)")
  }
}

guard let identifier = NSBundle.mainBundle().bundleIdentifier else {
  fatalError("BundleIdentifier is nil")
}
options[NSPersistentStoreUbiquitousContentNameKey] = identifier
options[NSPersistentStoreUbiquitousContentURLKey] = cloudURL

do {
  try psc.migratePersistentStore(store!, toURL: storeURL,
    options: options, withType: NSSQLiteStoreType)
} catch {
  fatalError("Failed to migrate store: \(error)")
}

if let closure = self.initializationComplete {
  dispatch_async(dispatch_get_main_queue()) {
    closure()
  }
}
```

Now we come to the more complicated decision. iCloud is enabled, but we don't know whether a migration is needed. First, we go ahead and complete the storeURL with the "new" filename, PPRecipes-iCloud.sqlite. Next, we construct the "old" file URL for PPRecipes.sqlite. If the "old" URL exists (via the NSFileManager), then we need to perform a migration. We add the "old" file to the NSPersistentStore-Coordinator and obtain a reference to the NSPersistentStore. Once we confirm that it was loaded successfully, we can proceed with the migration. Since we want the "new" store to be connected to iCloud, we now need to add in the options for iCloud configuration to our options dictionary. These are the options we discussed in *Configuring iCloud*, on page 130. Once the options dictionary has been updated, we can kick off the migration via a call to -migratePersistentStore: toURL: options: withType: error:. This call does several things:

- Creates a new SQLite file at the location specified by storeURL

- Copies all the data from the "old" file to the "new" file

- Registers the "new" file with iCloud per the options that are specified in the dictionary

- Removes the "old" store from the NSPersistentStoreCoordinator

- Adds the "new" SQLite file to the NSPersistentStoreCoordinator

It's a lot of work for one line of code, and keep in mind that this line of code can take some time. Therefore, depending on our user experience, we may want to broadcast a notification before the work begins so our user interface updates and lets the user know what's going on.

Assuming the migration was successful, we have to delete the old SQLite file from disk so we don't accidentally repeat these steps on the next launch.

Once the migration and the deletion are complete, we're finally ready to notify the UIApplicationDelegate that the Core Data stack is ready for use.

Desktop iCloud Integration

So far in this chapter we've focused primarily on iOS; the reason is that the desktop implementation is actually a subset of the iOS implementation. There's no UIManagedDocument on the desktop. As a result, we must use the traditional Core Data stack and add the options to the NSPersistentStoreCoordinator ourselves. Even if we're using an NSPersistentDocument, we must still handle adding the options for the NSPersistentStoreCoordinator.

To build a new Core Data desktop application and implement iCloud data syncing, refer to *Direct NSManagedObjectContext to iCloud*, on page 129 for information, because the steps are identical. Further, to migrate an existing desktop application that uses a traditional Core Data stack, refer to *Migrating an Existing Application*, on page 135, because that's also identical.

If we're using an NSPersistentDocument, things get a little interesting—not a lot but enough to merit attention. The first thing we need to do is to subclass NSPersistentDocument. The reason for this is that unlike with UIManagedDocument, there's no way to pass in options to the NSPersistentStore when it's being added to the NSPersistentStoreCoordinator. That's the reason for subclassing.

iCloud/PPRecipes/MyDocument.swift

```swift
override func configurePersistentStoreCoordinatorForURL(url: NSURL,
  ofType fileType: String, modelConfiguration configuration: String?,
  storeOptions: [String : AnyObject]?) throws {

  var options = [String:AnyObject]()
  if let inStoreOptions = storeOptions {
    for (key, value) in inStoreOptions {
      options[key] = value
    }
  }

  let fileMan = NSFileManager.defaultManager()
  if let cloudURL = fileMan.URLForUbiquityContainerIdentifier(nil),
    let pathComp = url.lastPathComponent,
    let identifier = NSBundle.mainBundle().bundleIdentifier {

    let finalURL = cloudURL.URLByAppendingPathComponent(pathComp)
    options[NSPersistentStoreUbiquitousContentNameKey] = identifier
    options[NSPersistentStoreUbiquitousContentURLKey] = finalURL

  } else {
    fatalError("Missing component to initialize persistent store")
  }

  return try super.configurePersistentStoreCoordinatorForURL(url,
    ofType: fileType, modelConfiguration: configuration,
    storeOptions: options)
}
```

In this override, we first check to see whether iCloud is enabled. If it is, we build our full iCloud URL and then add the two options required to link our persistent store with iCloud. Once the options dictionary has been updated, we return control to our super's implementation.

In this example, we take the lastPathComponent from the URL and use it as our unique sandbox within iCloud. Depending on the application's design, this may not be unique enough, so we might want to consider storing a GUID inside of the metadata of the NSPersistentStore and using that as the unique identifier within iCloud.

Once the initialization has been completed and linked to iCloud, all of the other behavior is the same between iOS and Mac OS X. We can listen for notifications about iCloud merging data into Core Data and handle those merges in the same way.

Issues with Data Quantities

As discussed in *Under the Hood*, on page 133, Core Data uses transaction logs to keep multiple persistent stores in sync with each other. Because of that design and because of the latency of networking, there's an upper limit to the frequency in which we can create entities and save them to our Core Data application. The exact numbers are difficult to determine, but it's safe to say that if we're generating hundreds of entities per save, we may run into a performance problem.

Whenever we create an NSManagedObject and save the NSManagedObjectContext or the UIManagedDocument, a transaction log is created for that instance. The more entities we create, the larger that transaction log becomes. There's an upper threshold whereby the creation/transmission of transaction logs is unable to keep up with the frequency of entities being generated. When that threshold is hit, iCloud syncing is unable to keep up with the data generation and eventually fails. This failure usually results in a crash in your application.

Unfortunately, there's no magic number of entities to keep under. The threshold is a combination of processor speed, number of entities, size of the entities, and network speed. The slower the processor and/or network, then the fewer entities that are needed to reach the threshold. As an example, using an iPhone 4S on a performant Wi-Fi connection, it was possible to reach this threshold by generating a new entity every second with minimal size. With larger entities or a poorer network, it'd be possible to reach the threshold with fewer entities.

At this time, there's no known workaround for this issue other than to decrease the amount of data that's being pushed to iCloud. The amount of data can be decreased by generating less data or by "rolling up" the data into fewer entities. Ideally, this issue will be resolved at some point soon.

Sharing Data Between iOS and OS X

So far, we've discussed sharing data between iOS devices and linking our OS X application to iCloud. However, we haven't discussed how to share data between OS X and iOS. Fortunately, there's virtually no difference between

OS X and iOS iCloud integration, though there are a couple of rules that we need to follow.

The Content Name Key Must Be the Same

The NSPersistentStoreUbiquitousContentNameKey is the unique value that iCloud uses to determine what data we're accessing. If two devices use the same value and are signed by the same developer, they'll be able to access the same data. If one or more devices and one or more OS X machines use the same key, they'll share the same data. Throughout these examples, we've been using the value [[NSBundle mainBundle] bundleIdentifier]. There's nothing wrong with using that value, so long as all of our applications are using the same bundle identifier. However, if they aren't, we must use a different string to serve as this key. Apple recommends a reverse DNS notation style, and I certainly see no reason to suggest otherwise.

The Data Model Must Be the Same

Core Data is virtually identical between iOS and OS X. We can use the same data model, even the same file, between OS X and iOS. iCloud expects and requires us to do exactly that. If the data models don't match, the transaction logs can't be played back properly, and the synchronizing fails. The easiest way to ensure this is to share the data model (and the entity subclasses) between the OS X application and the iOS application. This step guarantees the applications are using the same model.

However, we must take additional care when upgrading the model. If we release an update to our iOS application but not our OS X application, they can become out of sync, and iCloud integration will stop working. Once the first device with a new model touches iCloud, iCloud works only with devices that are using the updated model. Any device using the older model simply stops working with iCloud. Fortunately, as soon as the out-of-date machine updates to the latest model, iCloud starts working again.

The best way to test iCloud syncing is to have more than one application running at the same time that uses the data. We could run our existing application on an iPhone and an iPad to see the syncing work, but watching the data sync between an iOS device and an OS X machine is far more interesting. To do that, we must build an OS X client, which is what we're going to do in Chapter 10, *Adding a Desktop Foundation*, on page 143.

Wrapping Up

iCloud is an incredibly powerful feature of iOS/OS X and Core Data. Although it's not perfect yet, it's going to continue to improve iteratively. It's usable in its present form on iOS 6.0 and OS X 10.8. As users get more comfortable using mobile devices, they're going to expect applications to sync across them.

iCloud is the solution to that problem.

Up to this point in the book, we've been focusing on iOS because it's the dominant platform that Core Data runs on. However, Core Data was originally designed to run on OS X and the bulk of what we've covered so far works exactly the same on OS X. However, a few things are different, and we'll explore those next.

CHAPTER 10

Adding a Desktop Foundation

Until now, we've focused primarily on the iOS side of Core Data. Although nearly everything we've covered works the same on Mac OS X as it does on iOS, some differences do exist. In this chapter, we're going to look a little more closely at the Mac OS X side of things.

To examine Core Data on Mac OS X, we'll follow our familiar pattern, starting off with an application on which to base our examples. Since we've already created an application on iOS that can share its data through iCloud, it seems only fitting to develop a desktop counterpart to the application that can sync.

Our Application

Before we start building our application, here's a quick overview of how the UI will look and work. Let's look at our breakdown.

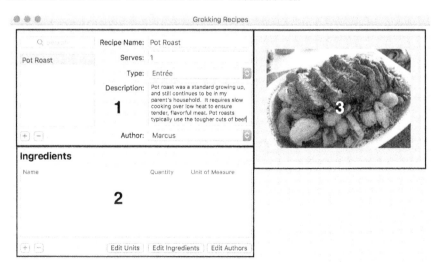

First, in section 1, we want to allow the user to edit information about individual recipes. The user will be able to select a recipe in the list and edit its accompanying details.

In section 2, we'll allow the user to enter the ingredients of the selected recipe. Each recipe will have its own list of ingredients that can be added, viewed, and edited here.

And finally, in section 3, we'll allow the user to add a picture of the recipe for reference. This is a view-only element, and the addition of the image will be handled through the main menu.

Our Application Design

For our revised desktop application, we're going to start at the very beginning. We'll launch Xcode and proceed through the steps to create the application and bring it to a usable state. At the end of this chapter, you may be surprised that so few steps are needed to create our Mac OS X application. This ease and efficiency are part of the allure and strength of Cocoa development. Coupled with Core Data, the efficiency is doubled. While we may be used to fairly quick development on iOS, Mac OS X is still easier and quicker to build for—at least up to the prototype stage. Once we have our prototype built and have confirmed that we can do what we want with the application, then all of the "little" things start to become obvious. This is often, lovingly, referred to as "the second 80 percent."

Sharing the Data Model

Since we've already developed our application for iOS, we want to leverage as much of that knowledge as possible. With Core Data, that leveraging is extensive. The xcdatamodel file structure is identical between Mac OS X and iOS. This means we can use the same data model we've been using on iOS. Further, since the data model can be shared and reused, we can share and reuse the data objects as well.

As of this writing, Xcode constructs projects so that the .xcodeproj file is above all of the other files needed in the project. The purpose behind this setup is so we can more easily structure our projects to share components between iOS and Mac OS X. Therefore, we start our desktop project by creating a new project named Desktop. I suggest creating the new project in a temporary directory, perhaps on your desktop. Once the new project is created, quit Xcode. Using Finder, move the contents of the new project in with our existing project. We could further clarify things by renaming the projects, but our main goal is to share the data model and the data objects. The final result is shown here:

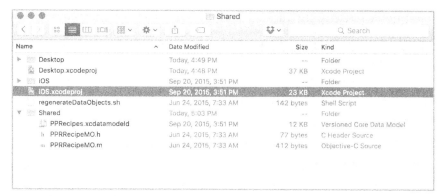

Once we have our data objects and data model in a position to be shared, reopen the Desktop.xcodeproj project and drag the folder into Xcode, adding it to the desktop project. Now our data model is complete.

Building the Controller Layer

As you may know from experience developing Cocoa apps, Interface Builder is a large part of any project. Now that we've built our data model and have a template ready in Xcode, it's time to put together the user interface.

There are two things to note before we get into the fun of Interface Builder. First, this isn't going to be Delicious Library. We'll be using standard widgets for our application to help keep the non–Core Data code to a minimum. Second, there are a lot of features we *could* add to this application, but we're going to hold back. Extra features, although useful, might detract from our current focus of porting the primary functionality from iOS to the desktop. Once we have that new foundation in place, we can start adding features.

The first part of the user interface we'll work on is the objects in the XIB file. As with most applications, we need to add the AppDelegate to the XIB so it will be both instantiated on startup and properly linked into the application itself.

Add the AppDelegate to the XIB

Depending on the whims of the templates within Xcode, the AppDelegate may already be in the XIB file upon opening MainMenu.xib. If it is, great! Move on to the next section. If it's not, we need to add it. In addition, please note that depending on the version of Xcode that's running, the application delegate could have the application name prepended to it. If it does, we must substitute that name with a reference to AppDelegate in this context. To add the AppDelegate to the XIB file, follow these steps:

1. Find the NSObject in the Library palette, and drag it to the XIB's window.

2. Click the name of the NSObject. When it's editable, change it to AppDelegate.

3. Go to the Identity tab on the Inspector palette, and change the class of the object from NSObject to AppDelegate.

4. Right-drag from the application to the AppDelegate object, and then select Delegate.

After these steps, the AppDelegate class will be instantiated when our application launches, and the application will send all delegate messages to it.

Adding the NSArrayController Objects to the XIB

We want our application to display a list of all the recipes in a single window. To accomplish this, we need to be able to reference the data so it can be displayed. So, let's add three NSArrayController objects into our XIB that reference that data. Our window will now reference those NSArrayController objects. Once the NSArrayController objects are added and configured, the XIB looks like this:

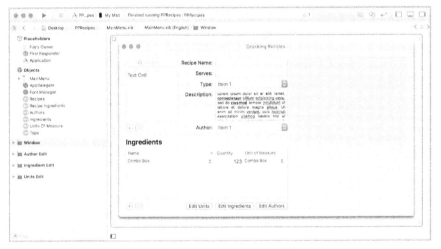

To add an NSArrayController for the recipe entities, follow these steps:

1. Find the NSArrayController object in the library, and drag it to the XIB file.

2. Click the name of the NSArrayController. When it's editable, rename it to Recipes. If you have trouble getting the element into edit mode, change the name in the Identity inspector in Interface Builder, and change the Label field in the Document section.

3. On the Attributes tab of the inspector, change the mode from Class to Entity, and change the entity name to Recipe.

4. Make sure the Prepares Content flag is selected.

5. On the Bindings tab of the inspector, bind ManagedObjectContext to the AppDelegate with a model key path of managedObjectContext.

Now that we have the Recipe entity's NSArrayController built, we need to configure the other two NSArrayController instances, one for the RecipeIngredient entity and one for the Type entity. The type NSArrayController follows the same steps as our Recipe entity, but we need to set the entity name to Type so it will populate with Type objects. Other than that one difference, we follow the previous steps to complete the type's NSArrayController.

Set the identity of the last NSArrayController, the recipe ingredients' NSArrayController, to RecipeIngredient. In the Attributes inspector, choose Entity, and set the entity name to RecipeIngredient. Set the bindings as before, with one additional change: on the Bindings tab of the inspector, enable the content set in the controller content and point it at the recipe's NSArrayController with a controller key of selection and a model key path of ingredients. See the following image.

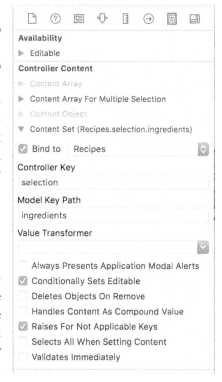

Now we're ready to build the NSWindow.

Building the User Interface

Now that we have all the data objects referenced properly, it's time to build the user interface. Although this interface won't be winning an Apple Design Award any time soon, it does allow us to view and edit all the data objects in our model. The window we're building looks like the following image on page 148.

Let's walk through the steps to set it up. For a more detailed review of this process, take a look at Chapter 11, *Bindings, KVC, and KVO*, on page 157.

Building the Recipe Source List

The first part of the interface we're building is in the upper-left corner, just below the search field. This view is an NSTableView configured with one column. It has no horizontal scroll bar, but it does have an automatically displaying vertical scroll bar. In addition, it has a hidden header and the highlight set to Source List. The scroll bars are configured in the inspector for the NSScrollView. The number of columns and the highlight option are configured in the NSTableView inspector. Each of the inspectors can be accessed by Control+Shift-clicking (or Shift+right-clicking) the NSTableView and selecting the appropriate view from the list. If the inspector isn't on the screen, you can display it via the Tools > Inspector menu item.

To bind this table to our recipe's NSArrayController object, though, we need to dig down a little bit and get a hold of the NSTableColumn so we can tell that column what to display. We could click in the table view until eventually we select the NSTableColumn, but fortunately there's an easier way. As mentioned, if we Shift+right-click the table, we're presented with a pop-up listing of all of the views; we can then select the NSTableColumn as shown in the following image on page 149.

With the NSTableColumn selected, we open its Bindings tab in the inspector and bind its value to the recipe's NSArrayController with a controller key of arrangedObjects and a model key path of name. Once this is set, our Recipe entities show up in

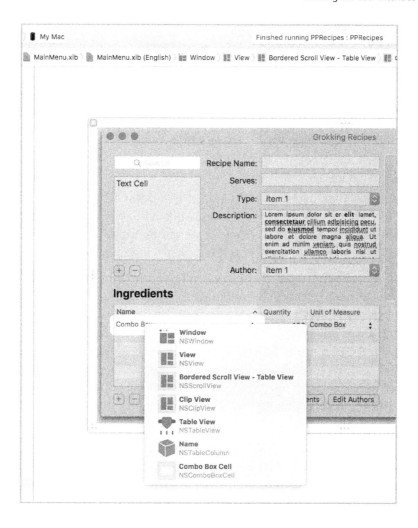

this table. More importantly, when we click a recipe in this list, the recipe becomes the selection that feeds the rest of the UI.

Let's add the buttons that will control the creation and removal of Recipe entities. For this step, we drag an NSButton (it doesn't matter which one) from the library and place it below the Recipe table view. In the button's Attributes tab, we set its image to NSAddTemplate (a system-level image available for our use), change its style to Round Rect, and remove its title if it has one. In addition, we must select the menu item Layout > Size to Fit to get the button to the perfect size. Once these steps have been taken for the add button, select Edit > Duplicate from the main menu to create a second button, and change the second button's image to NSRemoveTemplate.

Next, we can "wire up" the buttons under the NSTableView and connect them directly to the recipe's NSArrayController. The add button will be connected to the add: action, and the remove button will be connected to the remove: action on the recipe's NSArrayController. These buttons can be connected to their actions by holding down the Control key, clicking the button, and dragging from the selector sent action to the NSArrayController. With these small changes, we can now add and remove recipe entities at will.

Adding the Recipe Details

Now that the source list in place, it's time to add the details about the recipe. These details (the name, serves, desc, and type) tie to the now-valid selection controller key on the recipe's NSArrayController. As a result, when a user clicks in the list, the relevant details of the recipe are selected.

The first two items are text fields, the third and fifth elements are pop-up boxes, and the final element is a text area. With the exception of the pop-up boxes for the type and author, these details are configured in a very similar way. All of them have a value binding associated with the recipe's NSArrayController object through a controller key of selection and a model key path of name, serves, and desc, as appropriate. One tip with regard to the text area: be sure to turn off the Rich Text setting. When this setting is on, the field expects an NSAttributedString instead of a string, which can cause confusion. Additionally, in order to be good citizens, we should drag an NSNumberFormatter to the Serves text field and configure it to allow only whole numbers.

The pop-up boxes are a little more complex. Although each pop-up box is associated with the selected recipe, we need to populate the entire list of recipes with values. The values belong to other entities on the other side of relationships. While we want to, for example, show the selected recipe type, what we really need to display is the *name* of the recipe type being selected. Fortunately, this is a fairly common use case, and built-in tools are available to handle it. Each pop-up box is designed to be associated with an NSArrayController. And each NSArrayController references the entities we want to appear in the pop-up boxes. Furthermore, we can define each pop-up box to display a specific value from those entities.

We need to set three sections of values as shown in the following image on page 149.

- In the Content section, we bind to the type NSArrayController with a Controller Key setting of arrangedObjects. This step instructs the pop-up box to access the type NSArrayController for the objects it is to work with.

- In the Content Values section, we bind to the type NSArrayController with a Controller Key setting of arrangedObjects. We also want to set the Model Key Path setting to name. This step instructs the pop-up to access the name property for its display value.

- In the Selected Object section, we bind to the recipe's NSArrayController and use a Controller Key setting of selection. Further, we want to set the Model Key Path setting to type. This instructs the pop-up to do several things. First, it checks the selected recipe for its type relationship and displays the value associated. Second, it updates the selected recipe when a user selects a different value in the Type pop-up list. And finally, it monitors the recipe NSArrayController and updates itself if the user selects a different recipe.

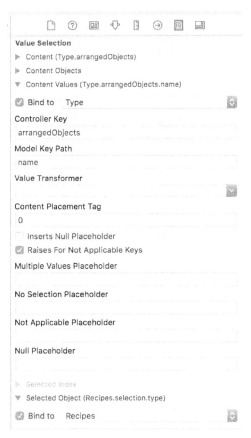

Once we have the Type pop-up box set, we need to configure the Author pop-up box. The setup here is identical to that for the Type pop-up box, except the NSArrayController to use is the author NSArrayController, and the Selected Object Model Key Path setting will be author.

Adding the Ingredients

Now that the recipe section of our UI is complete, it's time to add ingredients. The ingredients make up the table in the lower-left corner of our window. Fortunately, this part is almost identical to setting up the recipe source list. However, unlike the recipe source list, our NSTableView will have three columns, display its headers and its vertical scroll bar, and hide the horizontal scroll bar. We enter the column headings as Name, Quantity, and Unit of Measure.

Just as we did in the recipe source list, we bind the values for each column in the NSTableView to our recipe ingredients' NSArrayController using the controller key arrangedObjects and using the appropriate model key paths: name, quantity, and unitOfMeasure. The Quantity column (or, more specifically, the table cell in the Quantity column) should also have an NSNumberFormatter assigned to it so that the quantity is properly formatted for the value that it holds. Once those are configured, we can see the recipe ingredients for the selected recipe. Remember that we configured the recipe ingredients' NSArrayController to feed off the selected recipe, so we don't have to do anything extra at this point.

Like in the recipe source list, the add and subtract buttons are configured by binding them to the recipe ingredients' NSArrayController objects (the add: and remove: methods, respectively). And with that, the ingredients section is complete, and we're nearly done with our UI.

Adding a Splash of Code

Wondering where the code is? As it stands, our recipe application is fully functional. We can run it without any actual code on our part and start inputting recipes immediately. The combination of Cocoa and Core Data makes it possible for us to produce this application with no custom code. However, we're not stopping there.

Displaying a Picture of the Recipe

Since our iOS counterpart is capable of taking and displaying pictures, it seems only fair that the desktop variant should be able to add and display images. Fortunately, from the UI point of view, this functionality is an easy addition. Drag an NSImageView (aka Image Well) onto our window, and connect its Value Path setting to the imagePath of the recipe's NSArrayController with a controller key of selection.

Importing Images

Once we add the NSImageView to our user interface, we need to make our AppDelegate aware of it. In addition, we need to add a way to *set* the image path of our Recipe entities. Therefore, we must update our AppDelegate.swift and add an IBOutlet for the recipe NSArrayController and an IBAction to be able to set the image path.

Shared/Desktop/PPRecipes/AppDelegate.swift

```
@IBOutlet var imageView: NSImageView? = nil
@IBOutlet var recipeArrayController: NSArrayController? = nil
@IBOutlet var window: NSWindow? = nil
```

The @IBAction, specifically @IBAction func addImage(sender: AnyObject), is called from our main menu and displays an open file dialog box. Along with this step, we need a reference to the selected recipe in order to work with the Recipe entities. To accomplish this, we add a reference to the recipe's NSArrayController that's instantiated in our nib within the AppDelegate. Once the recipe's NSArrayController has been added to the AppDelegate header, we need to go back to Interface Builder briefly and Control+drag from the AppDelegate to the recipe's NSArrayController to complete the binding.

While we're here, let's add a menu item to the File menu that will allow the user to add an image for the recipe. We do this by making sure the MainMenu element is open in Interface Builder (it appears as a floating menu) and clicking its File menu. Next, we can either add a new NSMenuItem or use one that already exists that's not being used. Since the Save As menu item isn't relevant to our application, let's go ahead and rename it Add Recipe Image. Once it's renamed, Control+drag it to the AppDelegate, and bind the menu item to the IBAction we defined in the header, as shown in the following figure on page 154.

Shared/Desktop/PPRecipes/AppDelegate.swift

```
@IBAction func addImage(sender: AnyObject) {
  let openPanel = NSOpenPanel()
  openPanel.canChooseDirectories = false
  openPanel.canCreateDirectories = false
  openPanel.allowsMultipleSelection = false

  guard let window = window else {
    fatalError("mainWindow is nil")
  }
  guard let recipe = recipeArrayController?.selectedObjects.last else {
    fatalError("No recipe selected")
  }
```

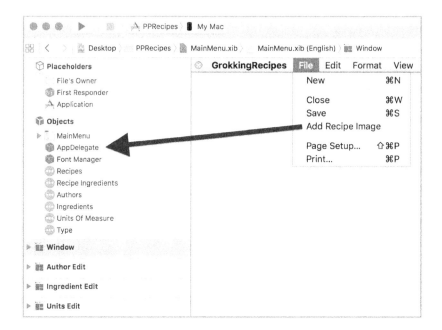

With the bindings in place, it's time to implement the addImage: method.

The implementation of addImage: displays an NSOpenPanel, which attaches to the window as a sheet, making it modal to the window. Next, we tweak the NSOpenPanel a little bit so it cannot select directories or multiple files or create directories. Notice that we check to make sure a recipe has been selected before we open the panel. Otherwise, without a recipe, we would have nothing to associate the image with. A little bit of error checking can go a long way.

Since sheets work asynchronously, we need to add a completion block. The completion block will be called once the user is done interacting with the NSOpenPanel.

Shared/Desktop/PPRecipes/AppDelegate.swift

```swift
openPanel.beginSheetModalForWindow(window) { (result) in
  if result == NSFileHandlingPanelCancelButton { return }
  guard let fileURL = openPanel.URLs.last else {
    fatalError("Failed to retrieve openPanel.URLs")
  }

  let fileManager = NSFileManager.defaultManager()
  let support = fileManager.URLsForDirectory(.ApplicationSupportDirectory,
    inDomains: .UserDomainMask)
  let guid = NSProcessInfo.processInfo().globallyUniqueString
  guard let destURL = support.last?.URLByAppendingPathComponent(guid) else {
    fatalError("Failed to construct destination url")
  }
```

```
do {
  try fileManager.copyItemAtURL(fileURL, toURL: destURL)
} catch {
  fatalError("Failed to copy item: \(error)")
}

recipe.setValue(destURL.path, forKey: "imagePath")
}
```

Our first action in the completion block is to check whether the user canceled out of the panel. An NSInteger is passed in expressly for this reason. If the user did click Cancel, we simply return from the block, and no action is taken.

Once we know the user has selected an image file, it's time to bring it into our application. We know NSOpenPanel is configured to allow the user to select only one file, so we can grab the -lastObject from the -URLs method of the NSOpenPanel. We now know what image the user wants added. At this point, we could simply add the path to our recipe.

But what happens if the user moves the image? Or the image is intended to be temporary? To ensure the image is always available, let's copy it to a known location within our control and use *that* file path. To accomplish these steps, we grab the filename from the NSOpenPanel and construct a unique path within our Application Support directory structure. Next, we use the NSFileManager to copy the image to that location. Last, we set the new file path into our Recipe object.

With the addition of the image menu item, we've completed the initial functionality of our desktop application. We can now share our data model across iOS and OS X. This level of code reuse allows us to maintain both applications and share functionality with a minimum of effort. As we add functionality to one, we merely need to create the UI portion for the other.

Wrapping Up

While the main purpose of this chapter was to set up a desktop app, it also demonstrated how we can share code and data models between the platforms. When it comes to building applications that need to span the platforms, using Core Data reduces the complexity just that much more.

Coming up in the next chapter, we'll take a quick detour into the powerful features of Cocoa that allowed us to build this desktop application with virtually no code. In addition, we'll add iCloud syncing and some other features that are unique to the desktop.

CHAPTER 11

Bindings, KVC, and KVO

Cocoa Bindings provides a lot of the magic behind Core Data. It consists of a number of APIs and concepts that together allow us to develop our applications using the Model-View-Controller paradigm, without requiring a tight coupling of the three aspects.

Cocoa Bindings allows us to design views, controllers, and models that all expect data in a specific format, without requiring that we bind them to specific classes. This means we can use views in multiple places and swap out controllers and even models without the need for extensive recoding, if any.

In this chapter, we look at some of the key components of Cocoa Bindings and then delve into the specifics of how Core Data works with those bindings. The two primary APIs we discuss are Key Value Coding and Key Value Observing. These APIs are part of the foundation that allows Interface Builder to function. Between the two of them, they give us a tremendous amount of flexibility in our design. In addition, Core Data uses these APIs heavily in order to allow us to focus on the business logic of our applications, as opposed to the data layer. With the combination of Cocoa Bindings and Core Data, the amount of code that we need to write, and therefore debug and maintain, is drastically reduced.

While this chapter is primarily focused on OS X, there are some fundamental portions that affect both OS X and iOS. Specifically, KVC and KVO are available on both platforms. While the Cocoa Bindings discussed in depth in this chapter applies only on OS X, I highly recommend that iOS developers become familiar with these technologies as well.

Key Value Coding

Key Value Coding (KVC) is one of the cornerstones of Cocoa Bindings. KVC allows us to access the attributes of an object without calling the accessors of that object directly. Key Value Coding is implemented through an informal protocol on NSObject itself and is used mainly through the getter/setter pair valueForKey(:) and setValue(:forKey:).

valueForKey(:)

The method valueForKey(:) is a generic accessor that retrieves an attribute on an object. For example, if we had an object called Recipe and it had an attribute called name, normally we'd access that attribute via the following:

```
let myRecipe = ...
let recipeName = myRecipe.name
```

However, this requires specific knowledge about the Recipe object to exist in the calling method. However, with Key Value Coding, we can obtain this same attribute without any preexisting knowledge about the Recipe object.

```
let myRecipe = ...
let recipeName = myRecipe.valueForKey("name")
```

By itself, this isn't all that useful. However, there are huge benefits that aren't obvious on the surface. Here's an example of how you might better take advantage of this ability:

```
override func description() -> String {
  var string = "[\(self.class)]\n"
  let entityDesc = self.entity
  for (name, _) in entityDesc.attributesByName {
    string += "\t\(name) = '\(self.valueForKey(name))'\n"
  }
  return string
}
```

In this example, we utilize the NSEntityDescription class (discussed in greater detail in Chapter 2, *Under the Hood*, on page 13) to retrieve the names all of the attributes of an NSManagedObject subclass and generate a string for display in the logs. With this method, we can reuse it in every NSManagedObject subclass that we create, rather than having to create a custom -description method for each subclass.

There are a couple of things to note in this example. First, the target object isn't required to have accessor methods for the attribute being queried. If our target object has only an ivar or property for a name, it will still be resolved and retrieved properly. (*ivar* stands for instance variable, which is different from a static or local variable.) In addition, if the target object has neither an accessor nor an ivar, the target object will still have a chance to respond to the request before an error occurs via the valueForUndefinedKey(:) method. Lastly, all the properties of an NSManagedObject are queryable via the KVC protocol. What this means is if we have an NSManagedObject defined in our model, we can retrieve an instance of that object and access its properties without having to implement a *single line of code* in the target object!

setValue(:forKey:)

Dynamically accessing properties on an object is a useful skill, but it's only half of what KVC does. The other half is the ability to dynamically set attributes on an object in much the same manner that we can retrieve them. Normally, we'd change the name attribute on an Recipe object by calling the setter method.

```
let myRecipe = ...
myRecipe.setName("Yummy Cookies")
```

As in the earlier getter accessor, preexisting knowledge of the Recipe object is required in order to use that accessor without compiler warnings. However, with KVC, we can access it in a more dynamic manner.

```
let myRecipe = ...
myRecipe.setValue("Yummy Cookies", forKey:"name")
```

This call attempts to use the setter setName(:) if it's available; if it's not, the call will look for and use the attribute directly if it's available, and failing that, it will call setValue(:forUndefinedKey:) on the target object. The combination of the dynamic getter coupled with the dynamic setter allows us to manipulate objects without having to write accessors and without having to know (or care!) if they exist.

Key Value Observing

Key Value Observing (KVO) is the sister API to KVC. KVO allows us to request notifications when an attribute has changed. By observing attributes on an object, we can react when those attributes are changed. KVO is also implemented via an informal protocol on the NSObject, and we register and remove observers using addObserver(: forKeyPath: options: context:) and removeObserver(: forKey-Path:). These are the two primary methods, although there are other methods involved in the protocol, just as with KVC. If we wanted to observe the name value on a recipe, we'd add ourselves (or another object) as an observer for that value, like so:

```
let kPragProgObserver = "PragProgObserver"
let myRecipe = ...
myRecipe.addObserver(self, forKeyPath:"name", options:[.New, .Old],
  context:&kPragProgObserver)
```

This snippet of code adds self as an observer to the myRecipe object and requests that when the name value changes, the observer should notify self of that change and include both the old value and the new value in that notification. We pass along a context so we can ensure we're acting on observations meant only for us and that they are not accidentally intercepted.

We do this because it's possible that our code isn't the only code in our application observing a value, and this method may be called with the intention of being received by our superclass. To ensure that the notification we receive is in fact intended for us, we check the context that's passed in. After this code has been called, any time the name property is changed on *that instance of Recipe*, the observeValueForKeyPath(: ofObject: change: context:) is called upon self. We can then handle the change notification as appropriate.

```
func observeValueForKeyPath(keyPath: String?, object: AnyObject?,
  change: [String: AnyObject]?, context: UnsafeMutablePointer<Void>) {
  if context != &kPragProgObserver {
    return super.observeValueForKeyPath(keyPath, object: object,
      change: change, context: context)
  print("Attribute \(keyPath) changed from " +
  "\(change.valueForKey(NSKeyValueChangeOldKey)) to "+
  "\(change.valueForKey(NSKeyValueChangeNewKey))");
}
```

When the variable is changed, we see output similar to the following:

```
Attribute name changed from untitled to Beef Chili
```

When we're done observing a value, we can stop receiving messages by passing removeObserver(: forKeyPath:) to the observed object.

```
let myRecipe = ...
myRecipe.removeObserver(self, forKeyPath:"name")
```

KVO allows views to automatically refresh themselves from the model when the data has changed. When a view is initialized, it uses KVO to connect all its components to the underlying objects and then uses the notifications to refresh itself.

Cocoa Bindings and Core Data

The combination of KVO/KVC (collectively referred to as Cocoa Bindings) and Core Data reduces the amount of code that we're required to write by a considerable amount. In the previous chapter, we wrote almost no code to create and display our recipe objects. Nearly all the work that we did was in Interface Builder. In this section, we discuss each of the interface objects that we used and how they work with Core Data. How does this apply to our application? Let's review the user interface that we built in Chapter 10, *Adding a Desktop Foundation*, on page 143 and how we used KVO and KVC.

NSTableView

Our recipe application makes heavy use of the NSTableView. In the main window of our application, we have two table views: one to list all of the recipes and another to list the ingredients for those recipes. Whenever an application needs to display a list of items or a grid of data, the NSTableView is the element to use.

In an NSTableView, like in the NSOutlineView, we don't actually bind the table itself to the NSArrayController. Instead, we select each column individually and bind it to a property of the objects in the NSArrayController as shown here.

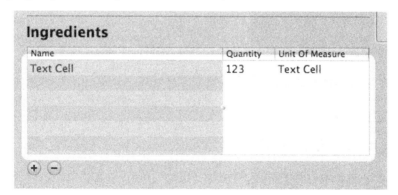

As we did in Chapter 10, *Adding a Desktop Foundation*, on page 143, we bind the column to the arrangedObjects controller key and the model key path to the value we want displayed in that column, as shown in the following image on page 162.

NSTableView, like NSOutlineView (as discussed in *NSOutlineView*, on page 165), plays very nicely with Core Data. This is especially true when the NSTableView is backed by an NSArrayController that's feeding the data. It's possible to use NSTableView with a custom data source, if that's appropriate for the problem at hand. However, when bound with an NSArrayController, the NSTableView can be

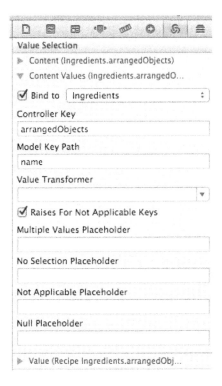

manipulated with other objects, such as the NSSearchView (discussed in a moment), to produce interfaces that integrate smoothly and provide a great user experience.

With this configuration, the NSTableView displays the data from the NSArrayController automatically and, thanks to KVO, stays in sync with the data stored in the persistence layer.

NSArrayController

NSArrayController is an extremely useful object when working with Core Data because it's aware of the Core Data layer and knows how to talk to it without any additional code on our part. When we configure it within Interface Builder, all that we really need to give it is the NSManagedObjectContext and a data object type. The rest of the work—retrieving the objects, updating those objects, and creating new ones—is all handled for us.

NSArrayController also understands relationships between objects when it's working with Core Data. In our recipe application, we have one NSArrayController configured to manage RecipeIngredient objects. Based on our data model, these are child objects that are bound to a specific recipe. Because NSArrayController understands these relationships, we can configure it to pull and display only those RecipeIngredient objects that are connected to a Recipe object that's selected in another NSArrayController.

This again is made possible by KVC and KVO. When we configure the RecipeIngredient's NSArrayController to provide only those ingredients that are related to the specific recipe, behind the scenes it's accessing the Recipe object and requesting its ingredients property via KVC. In the RecipeIngredient's NSArrayController, we bind the NSManagedObjectContext so that new ingredients can be added. In addition to properly being able to create (and remove) objects from the persistence layer, the NSArrayController will manage the relationship between the newly created or removed RecipeIngredient and the parent Recipe object.

All of this works because Core Data is the entire persistence layer and is accessed in a consistent way no matter what object is being dealt with. Because Core Data uses KVO and KVC, our controller objects don't need to know very much about the objects, other than the name of the objects and where they are stored. The rest is all resolved at runtime based on the settings that we provide in Interface Builder.

In our recipe application, we have one NSArrayController that is bound to the Recipe entity in Core Data. Because we also bound that NSArrayController to our NSManagedObjectContext, it's able to retrieve those Recipe entities automatically and make them available to the rest of the user interface. When our interface is loaded, those NSArrayController objects go out to that NSManagedObjectContext and ask for the entities that currently exist. Once they're loaded into the NSArrayController objects, any view element associated with them will be notified, via KVO, that the data is available for display. All of this happens behind the scenes; we're not required to write code for any of it.

NSFormatter

Users expect fields in the interface to accept their input and format it appropriately. This is where NSFormatter objects come into play. When dealing with any type of number, it's best to add an NSNumberFormatter to the text field or table column and define its display. Likewise, when working with dates, use an NSDateFormatter on the field or column to ensure the data is formatted and validated correctly before it's stored in the Core Data repository. When working with Core Data, it's sometimes necessary to manipulate the display of the data so the user's input can be validated and also so it can be displayed in a usable form. For instance, we aren't creating a very good user experience if we display currency as 3.99 versus $3.99 or display a date in raw seconds.

In our application, we used an NSNumberFormatter to display the quantity in the Ingredients column of our second NSTableView. If we were to add a shopping list to our application, we'd also use NSNumberFormatter objects to display currency and NSDateFormatter objects to show date and time information.

To add an NSFormatter to a field (either a column or a text field), select it in the Library palette and drag it onto the interface element. Once it's in place, we can configure its details in the Attributes inspector, as shown here. The Attributes inspector allows us to configure exactly how the data is presented to the user.

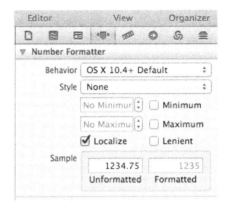

In addition to properly displaying number and date data, the NSFormatter classes accept input from the user and send that input back to the model in the correct format. For example, by applying NSNumberFormatter to the Quantity column of the ingredients table, we're guaranteed to receive an NSNumber back from the user interface.

Once an NSFormatter has been applied to an object, it can be a little tricky to reference it again to make changes. To change or remove an NSFormatter once it has been applied, select the number formatter in the element list on the left side of the Interface Builder view. Selecting the line item references the NSFormatter again so it can be manipulated. See the screenshot on page 165.

Other Interface Elements That Use KVO, KVC, and Core Data

Although the previous sections show how to access the Core Data repository in our recipe application with KVO and KVC, let's quickly review the other elements that, if we wanted or needed to, could be utilized to display the data in our application as well.

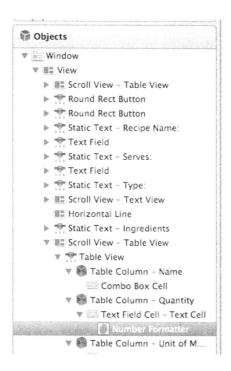

NSObjectController

NSObjectController shares a lot of similarities with the NSArrayController discussed earlier. However, unlike the NSArrayController, the NSObjectController is designed to represent *one* instance rather than an array of instances. A common usage of the NSObjectController is to represent the selected object of an NSArrayController, thereby making it clearer as to what data is being displayed in the interface elements that are bound to the NSObjectController, as opposed to an NSArrayController. Another common usage is to have an entire interface, such as a detail sheet or child window, be bound to the values within an NSObjectController and then have the File's Owner reference and populate that NSObjectController. In this design, the File's Owner (usually a subclass of NSWindowController) simply has to populate the NSObjectController with a call to content, and the entire UI is automatically populated. This again makes the maintenance of the code very easy and also improves readability.

NSOutlineView

If we wanted to change the look of our application, we could display a single NSOutlineView instead of the two table views we're currently using. With an NSOutlineView, we could display a list of recipes with a hierarchy of ingredients listed under them, as depicted in the following image on page 166.

NSOutlineView shares a lot in common with the NSTableView object. In fact, it's a subclass of NSTableView. The major difference is that the NSOutlineView displays data in both a column format as well as a hierarchical format. This changes how the data needs to be represented and accessed. Instead of a flat array of objects, the NSOutlineView expects the data to be in a tree structure. Fortunately, there's a controller designed just for that use: NSTreeController. Some care must be taken when working with Core Data and an NSOutlineView. In general, the NSOutlineView and the NSTreeController expect the data to be in a fairly organized state. NSTreeController expects each parent (or branch) to have children accessible via the same methods. This is a bit counterintuitive to having descriptive names for relationships between objects, and I normally implement accessors instead of making my relationships generic. For instance, if we had a recipe that has children named RecipeIngredients, I'd add another accessor to that relationship called children, purely for the NSOutlineView to use. We discuss custom NSManagedObject classes in Chapter 2, *Under the Hood*, on page 13. Unlike its parent object, NSTableView, the NSOutlineView doesn't work as cleanly as we might expect. We can combine it with the NSTreeController, but we get a lot more functionality and control by implementing the data source protocol for the NSOutlineView instead of using the NSTreeController object.

NSTreeController

As discussed in the previous section, NSTreeController objects are primarily used by the NSOutlineView interface element. Although they can store any data that lends itself to a tree structure, they're best suited as a controller for NSOutlineView objects. Unfortunately, there's still quite a bit of work to be done with the NSTreeController, and the results we get from working with it can be unexpected and unclear. Therefore, I recommend skipping it at this time and implementing the data source protocol instead when working with tree data.

NSSearchField

The NSSearchField interface element is an extremely useful tool and can provide an extra bit of polish to an interface. Its primary purpose is to filter the objects in an NSArrayController. That may not seem like much, until we remember that, thanks to KVO, any tables or interface elements associated with that NSArray-Controller will get updated automatically and instantly. This means if we put a search field into our application and link it to our NSArrayController of Recipe objects, our source list of recipes will automatically be filtered based on the user input into that NSSearchField. Even better, we don't have to write any code! All we need to do to implement it is configure the bindings for the NSSearchField.

To accomplish this, we first add an NSSearchField to our application. Here, we've decreased the vertical size of the recipe source list and inserted an NSSearchField above it. Next, we configure its bindings.

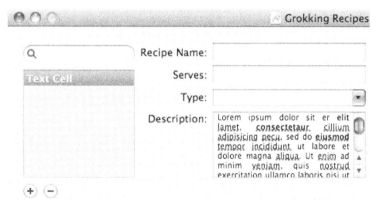

As shown in the following image on page 168, the NSSearchField interface element works with an NSPredicate. We write the predicate in the Predicate Format field, substituting $value for whatever the user inputs into the search field and using the controller key and value transformer to bind it to our data. In this example, we want to filter on the name of recipes; therefore, we bind the NSSearchField to our recipe's NSArrayController using the controller key of filterPredicate and a predicate of name contains[c] $value.

Once we add one predicate, another appears on the Bindings tab for the NSSearchField. This is so we can use a search field for more than one type of search. Each search will be shown in the drop-down on the NSSearchField, and the Display Name binding will be shown to the user. This allows us to create

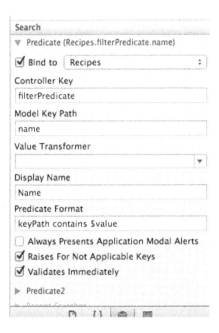

one NSSearchField that can search for recipe names, ingredients, descriptions, or anything else we may need.

Once the binding is complete, we're done adding a basic search field. Running the application shows that text entered into the search field impacts the list of recipes, as shown here.

Wrapping Up

Now that we have an understanding of Cocoa Bindings, KVO, and KVC, what else can we add to our desktop application that's specific to the desktop? In the next chapter, we'll look at additions to our application that will be used *outside* of our application.

CHAPTER 12

Spotlight, Quick Look, and Core Data

Developing for Mac OS X is about functionality meeting quality. When our applications have one without the other, we leave our users wanting more. They may not be able to define it, but "something" will be missing. Spotlight and Quick Look integration are two of those things that users don't look for when trying a new application but are pleasantly surprised by when they stumble upon them. Surprisingly, not a lot of developers handle this integration. Perhaps it's because Spotlight doesn't get along with Core Data very well. Perhaps the feature is too abstracted away. But one thing is for certain—integrating with Spotlight is the right move going forward. Spotlight is here to stay, and users will be using it more often and in more creative ways.

Unfortunately, for technical reasons, Spotlight and Core Data are at odds with each other. Spotlight works on the metadata of individual files, and Core Data stores everything in a single file. Because Spotlight is designed to work with the metadata of a file to discover things about the file, it won't work very well with a single-file design such as Core Data. When Tiger was first released, there were a number of applications (such as Entourage) that, because of their single-file design, didn't play nicely with Spotlight. In fact, Apple rearchitected Mail for that reason.

In this chapter, we'll integrate Spotlight into our recipes application. Once we're done, our users will be able to search for *Pot Roast* and find it in our application. In addition, when they select that search result, our application will not only launch but open to Pot Roast. While we're solving the Spotlight issue, we're also going to take a look at Quick Look. Although on the surface these two technologies appear to be completely different, they're handled in a very similar fashion by Mac OS X and the Finder. And although it's not 100 percent appropriate for our sample application (since we have only a single data file and that data file is hidden away in the Library/Application Support directory), it's very useful to understand how Quick Look works for document-based Core Data applications because it makes them easier to find in Finder, Spotlight, Time Machine, Mail, and many other applications. Lastly, Quick Look and Spotlight integrate rather well together. If our users activate Quick Look on a Spotlight result, we want them to see information about the recipe, not a picture of a generic file.

> ### Should I Just Use Separate Files?
>
> Throughout this book, the application we're designing uses a single Core Data file. This is done for the sake of clarity and because our focus is on Core Data. Depending on the application that's being designed, it's highly likely that it will be document based, and therefore it'd be appropriate to have one Core Data repository per document. In that situation, Spotlight and Quick Look can be a lot easier to integrate.
>
> However, for applications that are not document based, it's preferable to use a single Core Data repository, as opposed to individual files. Although individual files make Spotlight easier to work with, they'd be the tail wagging the dog. The main focus of object persistence (in other words, data files) is to quickly and easily access the data in a logical and reproducible manner. Core Data solves all those problems quite neatly—with the unfortunate wrinkle of not being fully compatible with Spotlight.

Integrating with Spotlight

The issue, as mentioned, is one of multiple files. Ideally, for our recipe application, we want one Spotlight "record" for each recipe in our Core Data repository. For Spotlight to work properly, we'd need one file on the disk for each recipe, along with its associated metadata. Therefore, to make Spotlight happy, we'll do exactly that. However, because all our data is being stored in a Core Data repository, there's no reason to store any data in these files. These additional files exist purely for Spotlight (and Quick Look) to utilize. Spotlight doesn't need any data in the files to work (it just needs metadata), we'll create very simple files and link them back to our Core Data repository.

The other gotcha with Spotlight is that the importer needs to be as fast as possible. What might be acceptable for processing one file or ten files isn't going to fly when Spotlight has to chug through thousands of files. Since the same importer that we're writing for use inside our application could potentially be used in a server situation, it needs to be as fast as we can make it. So, we're going to cheat a bit. Instead of looking up the metadata in our Core Data repository upon request from Spotlight, we'll store the metadata in the files we're creating for Spotlight. That way, our importer has to touch the metadata files only and doesn't have to initialize the entire Core Data "stack" (that is, NSManagedObjectContext, NSPersistentStoreCoordinator, and NSManagedObjectModel).

Creating the Metadata Files

We first need to produce and update the metadata files on the fly. To keep them as simple as possible, we just use plist files, as opposed to a binary representation or some other format. Since NSDictionary understands plist files, it reduces the amount of overhead needed for loading and saving the files.

To begin, let's create our first NSManagedObject subclass. This subclass handles producing the NSDictionary that will contain all the metadata. Since we're creating a subclass, we might as well implement some of the properties we'll be using to reduce the code complexity and make it easier to maintain.

Therefore, our Swift file looks like this:

Spotlight/PPRecipes/PPRRecipeMO.swift

```
class PPRRecipeMO: NSManagedObject {
  @NSManaged var desc: String?
  @NSManaged var imagePath: String?
  @NSManaged var lastUsed: NSDate?
  @NSManaged var name: String?
  @NSManaged var serves: NSNumber?
  @NSManaged var type: String

  @NSManaged var author: NSManagedObject?
  @NSManaged var ingredients: [NSManagedObject]?
```

We need to make sure we change the Class setting in the latest data model so Core Data uses our subclass rather than the default NSManagedObject as shown in the screenshot on page 172.

Implementing the Metadata Method

The goal of this metadata file is to contain just enough information to populate Spotlight and Quick Look but not so much information that the files become large and cumbersome. We must pretend there will be thousands of these files (even if in reality that would be impractical), and we don't want to impact the users' performance or their hard drive capacity. For our metadata files, we really need only the following information:

- The name of the recipe
- The number of people it serves
- The image for the recipe
- The last time it was served
- The description of how to prepare it

Most of that list is very light—just text. However, the image is probably too large to cram into the plist file, especially since we can't be sure how large that file will be. In addition, it would complicate the file format by including binary data. Therefore, we will put the path of the image in instead of the actual image. Because the image is stored on disk, we just access that copy.

In addition to this list, we need to add one more item that isn't user-facing. We want a way to link back to the recipe record in our Core Data repository so if the user tries to open the metadata file, our application will open and select the correct record. Use the NSManagedObjectID of the recipe and store its URIRepresentation (which is actually an NSURL) as a string in the metadata.

Spotlight/PPRecipes/PPRRecipeMO.swift

```swift
func metadata() -> NSDictionary {
  let metadata = NSMutableDictionary()
  guard let name = name else { fatalError("Malformed Recipe, no name") }
  metadata[kPPItemTitle] = name
  if let desc = desc { metadata[kPPItemTextContent] = desc }
  if let author = author, let name = author.valueForKey("name") {
      metadata[kPPItemAuthors] = name
  }
  metadata[kPPImagePath] = imagePath
  metadata[kPPItemLastUsedDate] = lastUsed
  metadata[kPPServes] = serves
  metadata[kPPObjectID] = objectID.URIRepresentation().absoluteString
  return metadata
}
```

Implementing the metadataName Method

Because we want users to be able to view the actual metadata files in the Finder, the filenames should represent the recipe rather than an abstract name. We use the name attribute of the recipe itself as the filename.

```swift
func metadataFilename() -> String {
  guard let name = name else { fatalError("Malformed Recipe, no name") }
  return "\(name).grokkingrecipe"
}
```

Generating and Updating the Metadata Files

Now that we have an implementation for generating the metadata per recipe, we need to add the ability to populate these files and keep them up-to-date. Ideally, we want to refresh the metadata files every time that the NSManagedObjectContext is saved. We add an updated save() method to our PPRDataController.

```swift
func saveContext() {
  guard let main = mainContext else {
    fatalError("save called before mainContext is initialized")
  }
  main.performBlockAndWait({
    if !main.hasChanges {
      return
    }
    let recipeFilter = { (mo:NSManagedObject) -> Bool in
      if mo.isKindOfClass(PPRRecipeMO.self) {
        return true
      } else {
        return false
      }
    }
    let deleted = main.deletedObjects.filter(recipeFilter).map {
      (mo) -> String in
      return mo.valueForKey("metadataFilename") as! String
    }
    var existing = [NSManagedObject]()
    existing.appendContentsOf(main.insertedObjects.filter(recipeFilter))
    existing.appendContentsOf(main.updatedObjects.filter(recipeFilter))
    do {
      try main.save()
      self.updateMetadataForObjects(existing, andDeletedObjects:deleted)
    } catch {
      fatalError("Failed to save mainContext: \(error)")
    }
  })
}
```

In this updated save() method, we're doing a couple of things before calling save() on the writer NSManagedObjectContext. Since the NSManagedObjectContext knows what objects have been deleted, updated, or inserted, we want to grab a reference to that information before the save() occurs. Once the save() is complete, that information is no longer available. Therefore, we grab a reference to the collection of deleted objects, updated objects, and inserted objects.

As part of this addition to the save(), we want to filter for just Recipe entities as opposed to every entity that's being inserted, deleted, or updated. By building a closure that filters for subclasses of PPRRecipeMO, we can filter each of the three collections and work with just PPRRecipeMO instances.

Because the deleted objects will be, well, deleted once the save() is performed, we want to extract the information we care about beforehand. To do that, we take the results from the filter and then run them through a call to map(), which returns a collection of strings from the collection of NSManaegdObject instances. In that map we call metadataFilename() on each instance to build the collection of strings.

As for the updated and inserted objects, the processing of the metadata is identical, so we filter both of those collections into a single collection that's ready to be passed on to the final step.

Once we have all of the information that we need, we go ahead and save the context. If the save fails, we just fail and let the application terminate. When the save is successful, it's time to update the metadata.

Spotlight/PPRecipes/PPRDataController.swift

```
if existing.count == 0 && deleted.count == 0 { return }

let fileManager = NSFileManager.defaultManager()

do {
  try fileManager.createDirectoryAtURL(metadataFolderURL,
    withIntermediateDirectories: true, attributes: nil)
} catch let error as NSError {
  if error.code != 518 { //Expected error
    fatalError("Unexpected error creating metadata: \(error)")
  }
}
```

Because we want to be in the habit of assuming nothing, we first check that there's something to update or delete. Once we're past that check, we need to confirm that the cache directory is in place, and either that our metadata directory is in place or that we can create it.

Spotlight/PPRecipes/PPRDataController.swift

```
for path in deleted {
  let fileURL = metadataFolderURL.URLByAppendingPathComponent(path)
  do {
    try fileManager.removeItemAtURL(fileURL)
  } catch {
    print("Error deleting: \(error)")
  }
}
```

The next part of updating the metadata is to remove any files that are no longer appropriate. Therefore, if the passed-in deletedObjects set contains any objects, we need to loop over it. Since we know that the name of the metadata file is stored in the deletedObjects variable, we append it to the metadata directory path and attempt to delete it.

Spotlight/PPRecipes/PPRDataController.swift

```
let attributes = [NSFileExtensionHidden:true]
for object in existing {
  guard let recipe = object as? PPRRecipeMO else {
    fatalError("Non-recipe unexpected")
  }
  let metadata = recipe.metadata()
  let filename = recipe.metadataFilename()
  let fileURL = metadataFolderURL.URLByAppendingPathComponent(filename)
  guard let path = fileURL.path else {
    fatalError("Failed to resolve path")
  }
  metadata.writeToFile(path, atomically:true)
  do {
    try fileManager.setAttributes(attributes, ofItemAtPath: path)
  } catch {
    fatalError("Failed to update attributes: \(error)")
  }
}
```

The last part of updating the metadata files is to process existing or new recipes. If there are new or updated objects, we then request the metadata NSDictionary object from the metadata method we created earlier. Using that NSDictionary along with the metadataFilename method, we write the NSDictionary to disk. For one last bit of polish, we update the attributes on the newly created (or updated) file and tell it to hide its file extension. This gives us the cleanest appearance when viewed inside the Finder.

There's one last situation we need to handle. If we have existing users and are adding the Spotlight integration after v1.0, we need some way to bring our users up to speed. Because this is a process that the user doesn't need to wait on to use our application, it's perfect to use a background queue.

Spotlight/PPRecipes/PPRDataController.swift

```
dispatch_async(queue) {
  self.verifyAndUpdateMetadata()
}
```

To do this, we add a check as part of the initialization of the Core Data stack. To avoid making the initialization function even longer, we reuse the existing background queue and do a single function call and put the rest of the logic in another function.

Spotlight/PPRecipes/PPRDataController.swift

```
private func verifyAndUpdateMetadata() {
  guard let path = metadataFolderURL.path else {
    fatalError("Failed to resolve metadata folder")
  }
  if NSFileManager.defaultManager().fileExistsAtPath(path) { return }
  let t = NSManagedObjectContextConcurrencyType.PrivateQueueConcurrencyType
  let child = NSManagedObjectContext(concurrencyType: t)
  child.performBlock {
    let fetch = NSFetchRequest(entityName: "Recipe")
    do {
      let r = try child.executeFetchRequest(fetch) as! [NSManagedObject]
      self.updateMetadataForObjects(r, andDeletedObjects: [])
    } catch {
      fatalError("Failed to retrieve recipes: \(error)")
    }
  }
}
```

Here we're looking for the metadata cache directory, and if it doesn't exist, we fetch every recipe entity in the persistent store and pass the collection to our metadata-building method. This also protects us from users who like to periodically delete their cache directory.

Creating the Spotlight Importer

Now that we have some metadata to work with, it's time to build the Spotlight importer. To start this part of the application, we need to first address UTIs.

Uniform Type Identifiers (UTIs)

Both Spotlight and Quick Look use UTIs rather than filename extensions to connect files on disk with (Spotlight) importers and (Quick Look) generators. A UTI is a unique string that identifies the type of data stored in a given file. I recommend that UTIs identify the company and application that created the data file, and like bundle identifiers, a reverse domain name is ideal for this purpose. (Note that bundle identifiers are in fact UTIs themselves.) Since our application uses com.pragprog.grokkingrecipes as its unique bundle identifier, we'll use the same UTI as the value of the LSItemContentTypes to identify the files.

Spotlight/PPRecipes/Info.plist

```
<key>CFBundleDocumentTypes</key>
<array>
        <dict>
                <key>CFBundleTypeName</key>
                <string>Grokking Recipes</string>
                <key>LSHandlerRank</key>
                <string>Default</string>
                <key>CFBundleTypeRole</key>
                <string>Editor</string>
                <key>CFBundleTypeExtensions</key>
                <array>
                        <string>grokkingrecipe</string>
                </array>
        </dict>
</array>
```

The UTExportedTypeDeclarations section is probably very familiar. Xcode generates it to describe any file that's handled by the application being built. The one difference is that, instead of defining a file extension (like txt), we're defining a UTI that's being handled by our application. This UTI is unknown by the system, so we need to describe it, again in our Info.plist file.

Spotlight/PPRecipes/Info.plist

```
<key>UTExportedTypeDeclarations</key>
<array>
        <dict>
                <key>UTTypeConformsTo</key>
                <array>
                        <string>public.data</string>
                        <string>public.content</string>
                </array>
                <key>UTTypeDescription</key>
                <string>Grokking Recipe</string>
                <key>UTTypeIdentifier</key>
                <string>com.pragprog.grokkingrecipe</string>
                <key>UTTypeTagSpecification</key>
                <dict>
                        <key>public.filename-extension</key>
                        <string>grokkingrecipe</string>
                </dict>
        </dict>
</array>
```

This key describes exporting our UTI and tells Mac OS X how to link it to different file extensions. In addition, this section describes the data to Mac OS X, telling the OS a descriptive name for the data type and where in the UTI tree it fits. For more information on UTIs, review Apple's documentation.[1]

Xcode Subproject

Our Spotlight importer is actually its own application. Xcode handles this with a separate project for the importer. (It's actually possible to include the plug-in as part of the main application project, but I've found that to be more hassle than it's worth.) Since we want to include the importer as part of our primary application and we don't want to have to remember to rebuild the subproject every time we build our main project, we'll set it up as a dependent or subproject within our primary project. To do this, we start by creating a project in Xcode and selecting the Spotlight importer, as shown here.

We want to save this project in a directory inside our primary recipe project, and we don't want to be too clever. We'll give the subproject an obvious name like SpotlightPlugin and include it with the Spotlight example project. To make Xcode build this plug-in every time we build the main project, we need to link the two together.

---

1. http://developer.apple.com/library/ios/#documentation/general/conceptual/DevPedia-CocoaCore/UniformType-Identifier.html

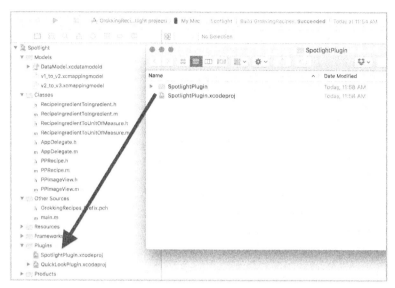

This is accomplished with the following steps:

1. Drag the subproject into the main project (shown in the previous image).

2. Open the target in the main project, and select the General tab.

3. Add the subproject as a dependency.

4. Add a new copy phase to the main project's target, and set its destination to "Plugins" and path to Contents/Library/Spotlight.

5. Drag the Spotlight plug-in into the new build phase (shown next).

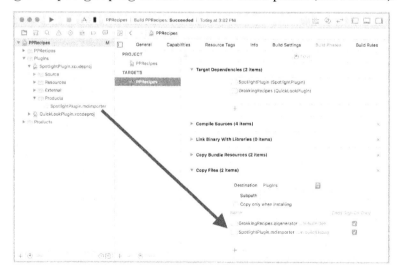

Now whenever we clean or build the main project, the subproject is cleaned/built. Taking this step also allows the subproject to be built with the same settings as the primary project.

Linking the Spotlight Importer to the UTI

With our Spotlight importer subproject in place, it's time to link the importer to the UTI for our metadata files. To do this, we need to update the Info.plist of our Spotlight subproject to let the operating system know which UTIs this importer handles.

```
<array>
<dict>
<key>CFBundleTypeRole</key>
<string>MDImporter</string>
<key>LSItemContentTypes</key>
<array>
<string>com.pragprog.grokkingrecipe</string>
</array>
</dict>
</array>
```

Here, we're defining our plug-in as having an MDImporter role, and the list of UTIs contains just the one for our metadata file. With this change, Mac OS X knows to use this importer to retrieve the information for our metadata files.

Building the Spotlight Importer

Now that everything is connected, it's time to build the importer. Fortunately, this is the easiest and shortest part of the entire process. The Spotlight template created the main.m file that we will be using, and it contains all the boilerplate code for us. The only code we need to write for the importer is in the GetMetadataForFile.m file. The template generates a GetMetadataForFile.c file, and that file will not accept any Objective-C code. Since I prefer Objective-C over straight C, the first thing I did was rename the c file to an m file. This tells Xcode to compile it as Objective-C rather than C. Because we'll be using Foundation APIs, we need to include Foundation.framework as well. As of this writing, it's not clear how to write either a Quick Look or Spotlight Plugin in Swift. Fortunately, the amount of code we're putting into these plug-ins is minimal.

Spotlight/SpotlightPlugin/GetMetadataForFile.m

```
#include <CoreFoundation/CoreFoundation.h>
#include <CoreServices/CoreServices.h>

#import <Foundation/Foundation.h>

Boolean GetMetadataForFile(void* thisInterface,
                           CFMutableDictionaryRef attributes,
```

```
                        CFStringRef contentTypeUTI,
                        CFStringRef pathToFile)
{
  NSAutoreleasePool *pool = [[NSAutoreleasePool alloc] init];
  NSDictionary *meta;
  meta = [NSDictionary dictionaryWithContentsOfFile:(NSString*)pathToFile];
  for (NSString *key in [meta allKeys]) {
    [(id)attributes setObject:[meta objectForKey:key] forKey:key];
  }
  [pool release], pool = nil;
  return TRUE;
}
```

The actual code for the importer is almost laughably simple. We're just loading the metadata file back into an NSDictionary, looping over the keys using the allKeys method, and adding each associated value to the passed-in CFMutableDictionaryRef. Once we're done with the NSDictionary, we return TRUE and are done. Since we're running inside a C function, we need to wrap the entire procedure in an NSAutoreleasePool so that we aren't leaking any memory.

Testing the Spotlight Importer

We can test the importer in a couple of ways to make sure everything is working properly. The first thing we need to do is generate the metadata files, which we accomplish by running our application. Once the metadata files are created, we can test the importer.

We can get a lot of information about our importer directly on the command line. Mac OS X includes a command-line tool called mdimport. A quick review of the man page reveals there are three switches for this command that are of immediate use. First, we need to tell Spotlight to load our importer.

```
mdimport -r ${path to our project}/build/Debug/GrokkingRecipes.app/
Contents/Library/Spotlight/SpotlightPlugin.mdimporter
```

Once Spotlight is aware of our importer, we can start querying it, again from the command line using the mdimport command.

```
cd ~/Library/Caches/Metadata/GrokkingRecipes
mdimport -d2 Test.grokkingrecipe
```

We can change the debug level (from 1 to 4) to display different quantities of information about the metadata file. If we use level 2 we can confirm the importer is working and get a summary of the data contained inside the file.

The other way to test the importer is to just search for one of our recipes! Click the spotlight magnifying glass in the upper-right corner, and enter the name of one of the recipes, as shown in the following screenshot on page 182.

But what happens when we try to open this file?

Accepting Metadata Files

Since we linked our metadata files to the primary application, Mac OS X attempts to open our application and pass the file to us. However, we have no way of handling that yet. We need to teach our application to accept a request to open a file:

Spotlight/PPRecipes/AppDelegate.swift

```swift
func application(sender: NSApplication, openFile filename: String) -> Bool {
  guard let metadata = NSDictionary(contentsOfFile: filename) else {
    print("Unable to build dictionary from file")
    return false
  }
  guard let objectIDString = metadata[kPPObjectID] as? String else {
    print("ObjectID was not a string")
    return false
  }
  guard let objectURI = NSURL(string: objectIDString) else {
    print("ObjectID could not be formed into a URL")
    return false
  }
  guard let moc = dataController.mainContext else {
    print("Main context is nil")
    return false
  }
  guard let psc = moc.persistentStoreCoordinator else {
    print("PSC is nil")
    return false
```

```
  }

  guard let objectID = psc.managedObjectIDForURIRepresentation(objectURI) else {
    print("ObjectID could not be formed")
    return false
  }

  let recipe = moc.objectWithID(objectID)

  dispatch_async(dispatch_get_main_queue()) {
    self.recipeArrayController?.setSelectedObjects([recipe])
  }
  return true
}
```

In our application delegate, we need to add the method application(: openFile:) -> Bool that will be called when the operating system attempts to open one of our metadata files. In that method, we load the metadata file into an NSDictionary and retrieve the URIRepresentation of the NSManagedObjectID. With the NSManagedObjectID in hand, we can load the represented Recipe entity and display it to the user. Since we want to return from this method as quickly as possible (the operating system is waiting on an answer), we display the recipe *after* we return from this method. To do that, we wrap the call to display the recipe in a dispatch_async, which updates the recipeArrayController with the selected recipe and allows the UI to update. By doing a dispatch_async and putting the execution block onto the main queue, we're effectively telling the OS to run the block right after the current runloop completes.

With that code in place, we can select a recipe from Spotlight, and our application opens with the correct recipe selected. The first part of our OS integration is now in place.

Integrating with Quick Look

There are two different ways to implement Quick Look. The application can generate images as part of the data bundle, or a generator can be written that generates the images on the fly. Storing images with the data is viable only if the data is stored in a bundle similar to the way that Pages or Numbers does. When the data is stored in a flat file, like our metadata files, a generator is the only way to integrate with Quick Look. Fortunately, writing a Quick Look generator is only slightly more complicated than a Spotlight importer.

Just like the Spotlight importer, the Quick Look generator is created within its own subproject.

Like the Spotlight importer subproject we added earlier, we need to perform the following steps:

1. Create a subproject under our recipes project. Again, I gave mine the very clever title of QuickLookPlugin.

2. Drag the project into the main project, and flag it as a dependency.

3. Add a new copy phase to the main project's target, and set its destination to wrapper and path to Contents/Library/QuickLook.

4. Drag the Quick Look plug-in into the new build phase.

If any of these steps are confusing, please see *Xcode Subproject*, on page 178. Once the Quick Look subproject has been added, the main project's tree should look similar to this:

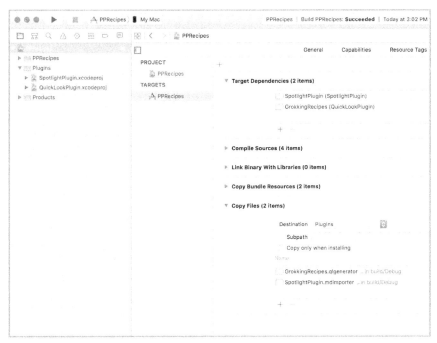

Now that the subproject has been set up properly, we will go ahead and rename the two c files to m files so that we can use Objective-C inside them. We also need to add Foundation.framework to the subproject so that we can utilize the Foundation APIs.

Unlike Spotlight, Quick Look has two components: a thumbnail generation and a preview generation. The thumbnail is used by the Finder both in place of a standard file icon and in Cover Flow. The preview is used when Quick Look is invoked in Finder, Mail, and so on. Therefore, the Quick Look template creates two c (now m) files, one for each. Let's tackle the thumbnail file first.

Generating the Quick Look Thumbnail

The file GenerateThumbnailForURL.m has one function inside it that's called by the Quick Look manager (part of the operating system). This function expects we'll be populating the QLThumbnailRequestRef and returning the OSStatus of noErr. Based on the documentation for Quick Look, even if we suffer a complete failure inside our plug-in, we should always return noErr.

As you can probably guess, our thumbnail generation code is going to be very simple. Because we already have an image included with each recipe, we're simply going to pass that image back whenever it's requested.

Spotlight/QuickLookPlugin/GenerateThumbnailForURL.m

```
OSStatus GenerateThumbnailForURL(void *thisInterface,
                                 QLThumbnailRequestRef thumbnail,
                                 CFURLRef url,
                                 CFStringRef contentTypeUTI,
                                 CFDictionaryRef options,
                                 CGSize maxSize)
{
  @autoreleasepool {
    NSDictionary *meta;
    meta = [NSDictionary dictionaryWithContentsOfURL:(__bridge NSURL*)url];
    NSString *pathToImage = [meta valueForKey:@"kPPImagePath"];
    if (!pathToImage) {
      //No image available
      return noErr;
    }
    NSData *imageData = [NSData dataWithContentsOfFile:pathToImage];
    if (!imageData) {
      //Unable to load the data for some reason.
      return noErr;
    }
    QLThumbnailRequestSetImageWithData(thumbnail,
                                       (__bridge CFDataRef)imageData, NULL);
  }
  return noErr;
}
```

In this method, we're again retrieving the metadata file and loading it into an NSDictionary. From that dictionary, we're retrieving the path to the image for the recipe and loading the image into an NSData object. From there, we call the QLThumbnailRequestSetImageWithData method, which populates the QLThumbnail-RequestRef. After that's done, we pop the NSAutoreleasePool and return noErr. From there, Quick Look uses the image we've provided whenever it needs a thumbnail for the file.

Generating the Quick Look Preview

The Quick Look preview is understandably more complex than generating a thumbnail image. If we do absolutely nothing for this part of Quick Look, we'd still get a rather satisfying preview, as shown in the following figure. But why stop there when we can do so much more?

Like the thumbnail generator, the preview generator is contained within one function call, and we're expected to populate the QLPreviewRequestRef and return noErr. Also, like the thumbnail generator, we'll always return noErr no matter what happens within our function call.

Unlike with the thumbnail generator, we aren't going to be working with just the image for the recipe. Instead, we'll generate a full HTML page that contains a large amount of information about the recipe and use that as our preview. Although it'd be possible to generate the entire HTML page in code, I'm rather lazy and would rather avoid that. Instead, let's take advantage of some XPath queries to locate the correct nodes inside a template HTML file, change the values to be appropriate for our current recipe, and use that to generate the QLPreviewRequestRef.

To start with, we load the metadata dictionary as we have previously. We're also going to load the image data into an NSData object again. Assuming there are no issues with either the metadata or the image loading, the next step is to set up the options for the HTML page.

For Quick Look to be able to use the HTML page that we're handing to it, it requires that we describe the document and include any attachments it has. This helps improve the performance of the HTML rendering, since it doesn't have to fetch any of the attachments. Therefore, in this section, we're setting up the properties for the HTML page, including specifying its encoding, the

MIME type, and the attachments. We also give it a display name that will be used outside the HTML page.

Once all the preliminaries are complete, we need to retrieve the HTML template from our bundle. Because this code isn't actually being called from our bundle, we can't just perform [NSBundle mainBundle] and get a reference to our NSBundle. (If we tried, we'd actually get a reference to /usr/bin/qlmanage!) Instead, we have to request it by its UTI. With a reference to the bundle, we can then retrieve the path to preview.html, which we'll be using as our template. Once we've loaded the HTML file into an NSXMLDocument, it's time to replace the placeholders in that file with real data.

We know the shape of the HTML document, so we can build simple XPath queries to retrieve each part of the document and replace its value component with data from our metadata in NSDictionary.

Once all the data has been put into the HTML document, it's time to render it and set the QLPreviewRequestRef. As this section of code shows, we're passing in the reference along with the HTML file as data and the property NSDictionary. When this is complete, we pop the NSAutoreleasePool and return noErr. Quick Look now generates our preview and presents it to the user.

Testing the Quick Look Plug-In

As of this writing, testing the Quick Look plug-in is a little more challenging than testing its Spotlight counterpart. Although we could use a command-line option to test it, getting the system to recognize the plug-in is a bit trickier. The issue is that the system tends to ignore what generator we want it to use and will use the generator defined for the system.

In writing this chapter, I used the following workflow to test the Quick Look plug-in:

1. Clean and build the main recipe application.

2. On the command line, execute qlmanage -r to reset the Quick Look generators.

3. Run the recipe application, which registers our Quick Look generator.

4. From the command line (can also be done in Xcode), I ran qlmanage -p ${path to metadata test file}, which generated the preview. Using the -t switch instead would produce the thumbnail.

5. Rinse and repeat.

After a few iterations the Quick Look plug-in will be used by the system. Fortunately, this isn't a situation that's an issue in production.

Putting It All Together

With a Spotlight importer and a Quick Look generator, it's possible to do some very interesting things in Mac OS X. For example, we can build a smart folder that finds all our recipes. We can then put that smart folder in the sidebar of Finder and easily access all our recipes directly from the Finder. Further, we can turn on Cover Flow for this smart folder and smoothly browse through the pictures of our recipes, as shown here:

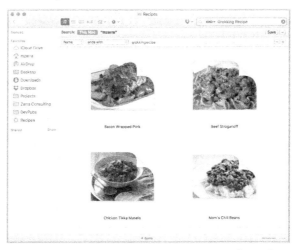

With the included metadata, this opens up quite a few ideas. For example, along with each recipe, we're storing the time it was last served in the metadata. We can use this information to further refine our smart folder to display only those recipes that we haven't served in the last thirty days. It's possible to get creative with metadata now that the operating system is aware of it.

Wrapping Up

With UTIs, it's possible to integrate even further with the operating system, Spotlight, and Quick Look. It's possible to publish a full description of the UTI—effectively injecting it into the tree and thus having the data type appear in Spotlight rules and more. However, this is beyond the scope of this book.

Here are some exercises you can try on your own.

Decreasing the Size of the Metadata Files

Depending on the application, it's possible to reduce the metadata files dramatically. Since the importer (and the generator) can stand up the entire Core Data stack, it's possible to just have the NSManagedObjectID (or even a unique identifier within the Recipe object) stored in the metadata file and have the importers and generators retrieve all the metadata information from the Core Data stack instead. (This is probably very similar to how Core Data does it internally.) This would also simplify the updating of the metadata—the only action required at that point would be to delete metadata files for records that no longer exist. However, take care with this approach because performance may suffer greatly.

Improving the Quick Look Thumbnail Generator

You may have noticed that we ignored the Max Size setting of the Quick Look thumbnail generator. That was done for the sake of clarity, and in a production system we should be sizing down the image to accommodate that setting. By doing so, we'd be good citizens and help the performance of Quick Look whenever our files are involved.

Document-Based Applications

When we're writing an application that uses a document model as opposed to a single repository, integrating Spotlight and Quick Look is even easier. Instead of having separate metadata files, we can simply store the relevant information in the metadata of the actual documents. This allows the importers to read the metadata without having to initialize the entire Core Data stack and still allows for very quick access to the relevant information.

Adding Spotlight and Quick Look integration into your desktop application gives it that bit of polish that subconsciously lets your users know they're dealing with a finished product.

Index

iOS 9 and Core Data

Delve into iOS 9, and the Objective-C version of Core Data.

iOS 9 SDK Development

iOS 9 gives developers new tools for creating apps for iPhone and iPad, and our new edition of the classic iOS guide is updated to match. By writing clean, expressive, and maintainable Swift code, you'll be able to pull in the iOS 9 SDK's enormous feature set to deliver mobile applications. In this completely revised edition, you'll work through an app's entire lifecycle, from creating the project to publishing on the App Store.

Chris Adamson with Janie Clayton
(342 pages) ISBN: 9781680501322. $42
https://pragprog.com/book/adios3

Core Data in Objective-C, Third Edition

Core Data is Apple's data storage framework: it's powerful, built-in, and can integrate with iCloud. Discover all of Core Data's powerful capabilities, learn fundamental principles including thread and memory management, and add Core Data to both your iOS and OS X projects. All examples in this edition are based on Objective-C and are up-to-date for the latest versions of OS X El Capitan and iOS 9.

Marcus S. Zarra
(240 pages) ISBN: 9781680501230. $38
https://pragprog.com/book/mzcd3

More for iOS

Unleash your imagination in two dimensions and get up to speed with the latest version of WatchKit.

Build iOS Games with Sprite Kit

Take your game ideas from paper to pixels using Sprite Kit, Apple's 2D game development engine. Build two exciting games using Sprite Kit and learn real-world, workshop-tested insights about game design, including cognitive complexity, paper prototyping, and levels of fun. You'll learn how to implement sophisticated game features such as obstacles and weapons, power-ups and variable difficulty, physics, sound, special effects, and both single- and two-finger control. In no time, you'll be building your own thrilling iOS games.

Jonathan Penn and Josh Smith
(216 pages) ISBN: 9781941222102. $34
https://pragprog.com/book/pssprite

Developing for Apple Watch, Second Edition

You've got a great idea for an Apple Watch app. But how do you get your app from idea to wrist? This book shows you how to make native watchOS apps for Apple's most personal device yet. You'll learn how to display beautiful interfaces to the user, how to use the watch's heart rate monitor and other hardware features, and the best way to keep everything in sync across your users' devices. New in this edition is coverage of native apps for watchOS 2. With the new version of the WatchKit SDK in Xcode 7, your apps run directly on the watch.

Jeff Kelley
(218 pages) ISBN: 9781680501339. $24
https://pragprog.com/book/jkwatch2

The Joy of Mazes and Math

Rediscover the joy and fascinating weirdness of mazes and pure mathematics.

Mazes for Programmers

A book on mazes? Seriously?

Yes!

Not because you spend your day creating mazes, or because you particularly like solving mazes.

But because it's fun. Remember when programming used to be fun? This book takes you back to those days when you were starting to program, and you wanted to make your code do things, draw things, and solve puzzles. It's fun because it lets you explore and grow your code, and reminds you how it feels to just think.

Sometimes it feels like you live your life in a maze of twisty little passages, all alike. Now you can code your way out.

Jamis Buck
(286 pages) ISBN: 9781680500554. $38
https://pragprog.com/book/jbmaze

Good Math

Mathematics is beautiful—and it can be fun and exciting as well as practical. *Good Math* is your guide to some of the most intriguing topics from two thousand years of mathematics: from Egyptian fractions to Turing machines; from the real meaning of numbers to proof trees, group symmetry, and mechanical computation. If you've ever wondered what lay beyond the proofs you struggled to complete in high school geometry, or what limits the capabilities of the computer on your desk, this is the book for you.

Mark C. Chu-Carroll
(282 pages) ISBN: 9781937785338. $34
https://pragprog.com/book/mcmath

Pragmatic Programming

We'll show you how to be more pragmatic and effective, for new code and old.

Your Code as a Crime Scene

Jack the Ripper and legacy codebases have more in common than you'd think. Inspired by forensic psychology methods, this book teaches you strategies to predict the future of your codebase, assess refactoring direction, and understand how your team influences the design. With its unique blend of forensic psychology and code analysis, this book arms you with the strategies you need, no matter what programming language you use.

Adam Tornhill
(218 pages) ISBN: 9781680500387. $36
https://pragprog.com/book/atcrime

The Nature of Software Development

You need to get value from your software project. You need it "free, now, and perfect." We can't get you there, but we can help you get to "cheaper, sooner, and better." This book leads you from the desire for value down to the specific activities that help good Agile projects deliver better software sooner, and at a lower cost. Using simple sketches and a few words, the author invites you to follow his path of learning and understanding from a half century of software development and from his engagement with Agile methods from their very beginning.

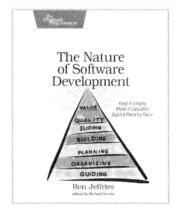

Ron Jeffries
(178 pages) ISBN: 9781941222379. $24
https://pragprog.com/book/rjnsd

Put the "Fun" in Functional

Elixir 1.2 puts the "fun" back into functional programming, on top of the robust, battle-tested, industrial-strength environment of Erlang. Add in the unparalleled beauty and ease of the Phoenix web framework, and enjoy the web again!

Programming Elixir 1.2

You want to explore functional programming, but are put off by the academic feel (tell me about monads just one more time). You know you need concurrent applications, but also know these are almost impossible to get right. Meet Elixir, a functional, concurrent language built on the rock-solid Erlang VM. Elixir's pragmatic syntax and built-in support for metaprogramming will make you productive and keep you interested for the long haul. This book is *the* introduction to Elixir for experienced programmers.

Maybe you need something that's closer to Ruby, but with a battle-proven environment that's unrivaled for massive scalability, concurrency, distribution, and fault tolerance. Maybe the time is right for the Next Big Thing. Maybe it's *Elixir*.

This edition of the book has been updated to cover Elixir 1.2, including the new with expression, the exrm release manager, and the removal of deprecated types.

Dave Thomas
(354 pages) ISBN: 9781680501667. $38
https://pragprog.com/book/elixir12

Programming Phoenix

Don't accept the compromise between fast and beautiful: you can have it all. Phoenix creator Chris McCord, Elixir creator José Valim, and award-winning author Bruce Tate walk you through building an application that's fast and reliable. At every step, you'll learn from the Phoenix creators not just what to do, but why. Packed with insider insights, this definitive guide will be your constant companion in your journey from Phoenix novice to expert, as you build the next generation of web applications.

Chris McCord, Bruce Tate, and José Valim
(298 pages) ISBN: 9781680501452. $34
https://pragprog.com/book/phoenix

Past and Present

To see where we're going, remember how we got here, and learn how to take a healthier approach to programming.

Fire in the Valley

In the 1970s, while their contemporaries were protesting the computer as a tool of dehumanization and oppression, a motley collection of college dropouts, hippies, and electronics fanatics were engaged in something much more subversive. Obsessed with the idea of getting computer power into their own hands, they launched from their garages a hobbyist movement that grew into an industry, and ultimately a social and technological revolution. What they did was invent the personal computer: not just a new device, but a watershed in the relationship between man and machine. This is their story.

Michael Swaine and Paul Freiberger
(424 pages) ISBN: 9781937785765. $34
https://pragprog.com/book/fsfire

The Healthy Programmer

To keep doing what you love, you need to maintain your own systems, not just the ones you write code for. Regular exercise and proper nutrition help you learn, remember, concentrate, and be creative—skills critical to doing your job well. Learn how to change your work habits, master exercises that make working at a computer more comfortable, and develop a plan to keep fit, healthy, and sharp for years to come.

This book is intended only as an informative guide for those wishing to know more about health issues. In no way is this book intended to replace, countermand, or conflict with the advice given to you by your own healthcare provider including Physician, Nurse Practitioner, Physician Assistant, Registered Dietician, and other licensed professionals.

Joe Kutner
(254 pages) ISBN: 9781937785314. $36
https://pragprog.com/book/jkthp

The Pragmatic Bookshelf

The Pragmatic Bookshelf features books written by developers for developers. The titles continue the well-known Pragmatic Programmer style and continue to garner awards and rave reviews. As development gets more and more difficult, the Pragmatic Programmers will be there with more titles and products to help you stay on top of your game.

Visit Us Online

This Book's Home Page
https://pragprog.com/book/mzswift
Source code from this book, errata, and other resources. Come give us feedback, too!

Register for Updates
https://pragprog.com/updates
Be notified when updates and new books become available.

Join the Community
https://pragprog.com/community
Read our weblogs, join our online discussions, participate in our mailing list, interact with our wiki, and benefit from the experience of other Pragmatic Programmers.

New and Noteworthy
https://pragprog.com/news
Check out the latest pragmatic developments, new titles and other offerings.

Save on the eBook

Save on the eBook versions of this title. Owning the paper version of this book entitles you to purchase the electronic versions at a terrific discount.

PDFs are great for carrying around on your laptop—they are hyperlinked, have color, and are fully searchable. Most titles are also available for the iPhone and iPod touch, Amazon Kindle, and other popular e-book readers.

Buy now at *https://pragprog.com/coupon*

Contact Us

Online Orders:	*https://pragprog.com/catalog*
Customer Service:	*support@pragprog.com*
International Rights:	*translations@pragprog.com*
Academic Use:	*academic@pragprog.com*
Write for Us:	*http://write-for-us.pragprog.com*
Or Call:	+1 800-699-7764

CPSIA information can be obtained at www.ICGtesting.com
Printed in the USA
BVOW09s1311120716

455253BV00007B/19/P

9 781680 501704